Light
in the
Middle
of the
Tunnel

edited by Irene Howat

Christian Focus Publications

For Margo

Irene Howat lives in Campeltown, Argyll, where her husband Angus is a pastor. She has written two books *Pain My Companion* and *When The Thornbush Blooms*.

© 1994 Christian Focus Publications
ISBN 1-85792-099-6

Published by
Christian Focus Publications Ltd
Geanies House, Fearn, Ross-shire,
IV20 1TW, Scotland, Great Britain.

Printed and bound in Great Britain by
Cox & Wyman Ltd, Reading, Berkshire

Cover design by Donna Macleod

CONTENTS

INTRODUCTION 4

1 MARION CRAIG 10

2 DOUGLAS FRASER 21

3 PETER AND TIM MAIDEN 34

4 PAULINE HILLIER 47

5 ALAN AND ANNE FRASER 60

6 IAN YULE 74

7 PRISCILLA MORGAN 87

8 DAVID SPRIGGS 97

9 RITA ARMSTRONG 109

10 DAVID AND RUTH KAY 123

11 ELMA ALEXANDER 136

12 KEITH JONES 149

INTRODUCTION

It is in the darkest night that stars shine most brightly. They do not change night into day but they pierce through the utter blackness.

This book contains twelve accounts of God's dealing with his children as they go through harsh and painful experiences. And it bears testimony that the light of the presence of Almighty God can shine in life's darkest tunnels.

When everything is going well it is easy to believe in a good God, indeed it is easy to forget about him altogether. But when things go wrong we turn to him for help and expect him to answer, questioning his very existence if he does not appear to do so.

Have we any right to do that? Did the people who share their stories in this book just turn to God when things became hard for them? Far from it. Each one is a Christian, saved from their sins through their best-beloved Jesus. And they have all discovered in their very different experiences that what the Bible promises is true. 'In all things God works for the good of those who love him .... neither death nor life, neither angels nor demons, neither the present nor the future, nor any powers, neither height nor depth, nor anything else in all creation, will be able to separate us from the love of God that is in Christ Jesus our Lord.' (Romans 8:28, 38-39)

These promises are made only to those who love the Lord. This book should encourage all who do and challenge any who do not.

4

Contributors

MARION CRAIG

Marion Craig went to live in Campeltown, Argyll when she married her husband Bob. They were blessed with four children and fostered over twenty others. But tragedy struck. Their youngest child, Harvey, died suddenly when only nineteen months old and just a few years later Ciaran, their eldest son, died after many months of illness. Beginning with a description of idyllic summers when the children were little, Marion goes on to tell with great sensitivity of the loss of her sons. Marion Craig's account of God's dealings with her family is written with the same dignity that marks her life.

DOUGLAS FRASER

Douglas Fraser was born blind. When only two years old he became a boarder at the Royal Blind School in Edinburgh where he remained for the next sixteen years. He has spent his working life in Glasgow. Apart from their involvement in their own congregation Douglas and his wife Cathie share an enjoyment of music as members of Glasgow Psalm Singers and their commitment to reaching the blind with the gospel through the Torch Trust. Douglas's story is one of an ordinary man leading an ordinary life. Take into account his blindness from birth and Douglas Fraser's story makes quite extraordinary reading.

PETER AND TIM MAIDEN

Peter and Win Maiden live in Carlisle in the north of England. They have three children - Becky, Tim and Dan. Peter is Associate International Director of Operation Mobilisation and also maintains a busy itinerant Bible teaching ministry. When Tim was in his mid teens he became ill with Crohn's disease, a problem which has caused him many problems since. He has not let illhealth interfere with his enjoyment of life which he lives to the full. Tim Maiden tells his story refreshingly and Peter allows us some insight into how his son's problems have affected him.

PAULINE HILLIER

Pauline Hillier has spent most of her life in the Bristol area. Ill health dogged her childhood and a lonely adolescence followed. Her happy but atheistic home became a sad and tormented one as her mother's mental illness developed and her father's lack of understanding compounded the problem. Pauline's story is dramatic and remarkable. Despite her childhood isolation Pauline grew into a 'people person'. Overcoming physical disability and emotional instability she became a church sister. In the course of her work Pauline Hillier has encountered many people in deep trouble. Her own early struggles have given her a special insight into their needs.

ALAN AND ANNE FRASER

Alan and Anne Fraser live in the Western Isles of Scotland. In 1973, when newly married, they went to Lima in Peru as missionaries. Alan taught in Colegio San Andres, eventually becoming headmaster. They had two daughters, then two sons. Some months after Donald, their youngest child, was born it became clear that all was not well with him. Alan and Anne tell us of the problems that Donald's mental and physical disability brought in its wake leading eventually to their return to Scotland. There is sadness in their story. Alan and Anne Fraser see Donald as a special child, their sadness was leaving Peru.

IAN YULE

Ian Yule is a member of a team ministry in Kirkintilloch. His special responsibility is pastoral. Soon after his marriage to Kathleen, Ian took up his first charge in Livingston, where their two children were born. Then came a move to Peterhead but his successful ministry there was punctuated by prolonged periods of ill health. After a very traumatic time Ian was diagnosed as suffering from Chronic Fatigue Syndrome or ME. He paints a graphic picture of the course of his illness and of the misunderstanding often surrounding it. His recovery was gradual but Ian Yule is now well enough to be in the full time ministry again.

PRISCILLA MORGAN

Priscilla Morgan and her husband are based in the north of England and it is from there that she pursues her career as an artist. But the development of her talent was fraught with difficulty. She was born into a small separatist community in which involvement with the arts was viewed with deep suspicion and profound discouragement. Priscilla capitulated to the pressure and suffered the emotional torment of someone amputated from herself. When the light dawned that her talents were gifts from God and to be enjoyed gloriously, Priscilla Morgan was set free to be a person, an artist and a success. (Priscilla Morgan is a pseudonym.)

DAVID SPRIGGS

David Spriggs lives in Inverness with his wife, Joy, and their four teenage children, Simon, Stephen, Richard and Emma. In his capacity as a clinical community dental officer, David serves a large area of rural Inverness-shire. In 1988, when he was 43 years old, he was diagnosed as having a fast growing tumour and David's condition was thought to be terminal. Now, five years on, he is in remission and well. Not only does he share with us a little of his experience of having cancer and undergoing treatment for it, David Spriggs also shares something of his wonder at still being alive.

RITA ARMSTRONG

Rita Armstrong and her husband Ron live in Clevedon. Rita's childhood was spent in war-time London and the trauma of those years bore fruit in bouts of mental illness. Having struggled to cover up her problems and be the perfect minister's wife, it was with a sense of relief that she learned that she was suffering from manic depression and that it was treatable. Medication helped enormously. But although life has been better it has also been hard as she has had to cope with the illness and death of one of her sons. Rita Armstrong discusses the experience of mental illness with disarming frankness.

DAVID AND RUTH KAY

David and Ruth Kay live in Barnstaple, North Devon where David serves as pastor of an evangelical church. In 1987, after working with a mission for several years the Kays left, believing that God was calling David from the work he was doing into the ministry. God confirmed that call six years later when they moved to their present home. David and Ruth share the 'waiting years' with us. These were not easy and tested their trust in God who did not let them down. David and Ruth Kay describe his faithfulness to them and to their growing - and increasing - family.

ELMA ALEXANDER

Elma Alexander lives alone with her cat, Benjie, in Crail in the lovely East Neuk of Fife. Still's disease affected her as a child and by the time she was in her teens Elma's body was stuck in one position and it has remained so ever since. Despite being totally dependent on others for all her physical needs Elma's account is one of remarkable independence. Through her love of Country music she has made friends all over the world. And through her love of her Lord Elma Alexander finds fulfilment and peace in what might otherwise have been a tragic life.

KEITH JONES

Keith Jones is Chief Executive of Mission Aviation Fellowship and is based in Folkestone. On completing his commission as a Naval Air Squadron pilot he and his wife, Lin, went with MAF to Chad and spent four years in Africa. It was after their return home, while travelling the country speaking about the work of MAF, that Lin developed leukaemia. After a long and difficult struggle Lin died leaving Keith bereft, exhausted and alone. By God's strength he began to pick up the pieces again and become involved in the development of the work of MAF. Keith Jones is now married to Ruth and they have a son David.

1

MARION CRAIG

Halcyon days

The summers of the 1970s lasted for ever. Or that's how it seemed when our children were little. There was never any question of 'What shall we do tomorrow?' The young and I were always on one or another of Kintyre's lovely beaches.

At the end of each afternoon even the smallest member of the family would help to brush the sand from the car and drag out all the paraphernalia of wind-breaks, fishing nets, spades and pails, towels and swimsuits to be washed and tidied ready for use the following day.

Thinking back to those carefree days I am reminded of the Bible verse: 'The city streets will be filled with boys and girls playing there' (Zech.8:5)

Ciaran, at seven the eldest, was always making things - the ideal Blue Peter child - ever seeking sophisticated equipment to create rafts and boats, telescopes and laboratories. At rock pools there was always a dam or an irrigation layout to be tackled. In winter the staircase bannister was the supporting structure for his complex creation of a cable car system operated by string pulleys which cut deep into the paintwork. Twenty years on I can't bear to cover the scars with fresh paint.

Next in line, at five, was Hilda, full of quick perception and an adventurous spirit which alarmed her older brother. Only for her had it been necessary to have an extra five inch section added to the cot side to prevent the agile little leg from levering her over to freedom. Along with her eldest cousin from next door she discovered that tummies very quickly reject the consumption of Granny's prize daffodils! She loved Ciaran.

Then there was Jeremy. At three he was a solid, sturdy, affectionate little figure whose constant companion was his 'Baba', a favourite cot blanket. It used to trail behind him on his travels until I decided that hygiene demanded better. So it was bundled up like a sausage roll, tied with string and clutched fondly under his arm.

One of the children's favourite expeditions was to the Bull Field at Machrihanish where we all scrambled down the Rickety Ladder and made our way along the path to the beach singing extremely loudly 'I love to go a-wandering along the mountain track.' Jeremy was borne on his father's shoulders and a podgy little finger stuck into each paternal ear ensured a steady ride. His stamina was inexhaustible. When only five he was in the lead as we cycled right round the island of Barra, frequently doubling back on his little bike with its fat wheels to see why the rest of us were pedalling so slowly uphill in his wake.

And lastly came baby Harvey. It was nice being the youngest, always having older siblings to interpret incoherent babblings and teach exciting things like throwing wet sponges out of the bath and drawing murals on the wallpaper. At the age of one he could recognise the signature tune of his favourite television programme, Barnaby the Bear, and would pad through to the playroom clutching Hilda's red handbag to watch from his own little basket chair. His vocabulary contained about six words. On a visit to the Wild Life Park at Aviemore the other children's apprehension when a large moose peered through the car windscreen was dissipated at the questioning tone of Harvey's 'Wow-wow?'

At about this time my husband Bob and I responded to a newspaper appeal for short term foster parents - in particular for new born babies. When our home was geared towards coping with tinies, one more really did not cause much additional work - the washings were enormous anyway and some extra nappies did not seem to increase the load. Our own children loved the new babies - at one time we had twins - and willingly helped to fetch and carry, to pat for burps and shoogle prams to soothe. Over the years we have had twenty-two little ones in foster care and are still using the original pram and carrycot.

Sudden sorrow

How were we to know that into this glorious bustle of family life was to come a sorrow so sudden and swift that we hardly had time to know what had hit us? Harvey became ill one Sunday in 1974 and was flown by air ambulance to Glasgow. He had contracted a virus, which, even after a post-mortem, was never identified. Only nineteen months old, he died within the week and was buried on my birthday.

Christmas followed a fortnight later so what does a parent do? Of course, the other children missed him but their innocent trust readily accepted that Harvey was safe and happy in heaven, and as far as they were concerned it was now time to open the brightly wrapped parcels under the tree. With aching hearts Bob and I realised that our responsibility was not to overburden them with our grief but to continue the process of nurturing and loving them. How conscious we were of the saying 'Life goes on'.

Life goes on
Living on the west coast of Scotland with its treasure-trove of beautiful islands and idyllic anchorages, the family spent many precious summer weeks on the high seas sailing our Westerly yacht - foster baby on board if the occasion demanded. In winter the family skied together - mostly abroad as Scottish weather was invariably too demanding for young children. On our few trips to Cairngorm, Jeremy's propensity for whizzing off the piste to land head first in a snow drift was no doubt good training for the hours he now spends instructing on that same mountain.

Music plays a large part in our family life. By profession I was a classical singer and over the years observed with delight as Hilda excelled on piano and trumpet while Jeremy attained the dizzy heights of 'A' level singing and tuba playing. I treasured God's gift of a voice which could sing and marvelled at the way he guided my career - opening the right doors and closing the wrong ones. I rejoiced at being able to communicate to others my faith and the gospel of Jesus Christ.

Becoming a Christian had not been difficult for me. As far back as I can remember into my childhood I knew I had a close and personal relationship with Jesus. Without doubt the way was made easy by the stable and godly home and sound teaching provided by my parents. Bob and I sought to do the same for our children from the moment they were born.

In 1981, I was to be soloist at a Crusade being led in Glasgow's Kelvin Hall by the evangelist Luis Palau. 1980 saw almost a year-long build-up for the event - on my part participating in concerts and Praise Rallies, held either in the City Halls or Kelvin Hall itself. When the Crusade was over, follow up engagements continued for several months. Planning and preparation went on apace and I thank the Lord that I did not know what lay ahead.

The bad dream

A week before the opening concert in 1980 Ciaran started having violent headaches and we again found ourselves thrown into the bad dream of air ambulance to Glasgow. I watched in disbelief as his unconscious, ashen-faced little form was wheeled into Intensive Care. I waited. I prayed. Surely it couldn't happen again. His operating surgeon diagnosed a brain tumour, highly malignant and fast growing.

With Ciaran we had more time to come to terms with the harsh reality that we were going to lose the brilliant thirteen year old of whom we were so proud - just about to enter Winchester College. After surgery and during the next year of chemotherapy and radiotherapy there developed a bond, a closeness which was telepathic in its intensity. Without asking, I sensed his every thought and need and knew that the security of my constant presence gave him the emotional strength to cope with each stage of treatment.

We have only the highest praise for his consultant, Dr Michael Willoughby, whose dedication to improving quality of life for his patients was tireless. He spent time listening intently to each child - and was more than taken aback when Ciaran announced one day that he felt his recovery was a case of 'Festina lente'. I don't think there were many children in Yorkhill Hospital for Sick Children who quoted Latin!

The hours, the days, the weeks spent in hospital were both heartbreaking and humbling. Help was always at hand but I had an overwhelming weight of sadness as I watched each family coping with their desperately ill child - hair coming out in handfuls and little bodies being blown up like balloons by steroids. Injections, blood tests, intravenous drips, violent bouts of sickness are the daily lot of dozens of precious little ones.

Ciaran recovered sufficiently to return part time to school and be dux of the year, to come sailing again and even to ski somewhat shakily. I remember feeling a surge of anger when a gruff ski-lift operator mocked us for helping our thirteen year old boy on to the chair lift and for carrying his skis for him. Of course he did not know the circumstances but Ciaran was so hurt.

In connection with the Luis Palau Crusade I was asked to make a record at an Edinburgh studio. My pianist, Esther McColl, was there; my organist, Bob Christie, was there; but above all my eldest son was there, his eyes sparkling with fascination and involvement as he absorbed all the technicalities of the recording process. He had no knowledge of my anguish as I sang:

When He shall call, from earth's remotest corners
All who have stood triumphant in His might,
O to be worthy then to stand beside them
And in that morn to walk with Him in white.

Ciaran's Christian faith was of necessity simple but nonetheless straightforward and real. With his apparent ability to remember everything he saw in print, his daily reading with the help of Scripture Union Notes had built up a considerable knowledge and understanding of the Word of God.

The very next day he began to lose his balance and choke when trying to swallow; so we hot-footed it back to Dr Willoughby. The tumour had spread. Massive radiotherapy retarded the deterioration into increasing paralysis and helplessness and when death came after six more months it was a merciful release.

God in the midst of it

There is no doubt in my mind that God, in his infinite love and wisdom, protected Ciaran from the understanding that death was on the horizon. His considerable mental powers manifested themselves from an early age and his grasp of mathematics, electronics, astronomy and everything in which he chose to take an interest was outstanding. He avidly questioned the theory and practice of radiotherapy, knew what all the chemotherapy drugs were doing and in human terms should have realised the severity of his illness. Never once did he contemplate that the outcome would be less than a complete cure. At each stage of his deterioration we were able to give him an explanation which satisfied and reassured.

His mind was active to the end and, although too paralysed to hold a book, he spent hours listening to story tapes. His favourite was the first of the *Chronicles of Narnia* by C S Lewis and, as I listened to the haunting harp music surrounding Michael Hordern's portrayal of the glorious voice and words of Aslan, I quietly wondered if the sense of peace and security was intentionally being set for my brave son.

On the morning of the day he died a letter arrived from a friend in Zimbabwe who was aware that Bob and I were nursing Ciaran at home. He wrote, 'Ultimately you may have to let him walk alone through the valley of the shadow until the sun rises over the hill and he sees the glory of God in a way that we cannot do and hastens on to rejoice in the love and presence of Jesus Christ, to an extent which we will never know in this present world.' And on that very day, that's how it was.

If we could only grasp how far better it is to be 'with Christ' (Philippians 1:23) and catch even a glimpse of the liberty and spaciousness of his presence, we could never be selfish enough to wish a return to the bondage and limitations of mortal life for those who have gone on ahead, however much we miss them and feel sad for the void left in our own lives. As the Christian view is that we are linked inextricably with the eternal God (Psalm 90:1), time should be seen as merging with eternity; and death, not as a barrier, a severing of relationship, but the gateway to the fulfilment of all that Christ has made possible for us through his death and rising again. The absolute assurance of these things and the confidence that though our children cannot return to us we shall go to them (2 Samuel 12:23), sustains, comforts and provides the will to go on.

Arising out of these experiences came a re-appraisal of perspective and priorities. Our two middle children, Hilda and Jeremy, learned to share and care and their own characters were refined as they came more closely into contact with Ciaran's uncomplaining and lovely nature, not at all warped or stunted by distress and frustration as his handicap progressed. Bob and I now know at first hand the emotional strain of maintaining a cheerful and positive attitude towards a child suffering from terminal illness, following doctors' advice to plan with him future events which we knew he would never live to see. We have a new respect and understanding for parents who ungrudgingly look after a handicapped child year in, year out, more sympathy for children confined to hospital for long periods, and infinitely more admiration for the dedication of doctors and nurses.

We have a genuine bond with other parents who lose a child and are able to display more sensitivity when speaking to them. When we lost Harvey we got, 'Will you have another baby to take his place?' That was intrusive. When Ciaran died the illogical comfort offered was, 'Well at least you still have two.' Harvey was Harvey and Ciaran was Ciaran and each was unique and irreplaceable. We were again also made aware of maintaining the testimony to our faith, for to 'crack' in practical adversity would surely negate our preaching and teaching and singing when all was going well.

The place of prayer

And what about prayer which has scarcely been mentioned so far? We were astonished and humbled by the number who told us they were praying for us. Some wished us good luck on hearing that Ciaran was so ill, others kept their fingers crossed, but most assured us that they were praying. Comparative strangers would stop us in the street and tell us so.

Sometimes I was so numbed with grief at having to leave Ciaran's bedside and drive 140 miles to sing at the Crusade that I found it impossible to pray. But both Bob and I were almost physically aware of the 'cushion' surrounding us, a cushion made up of the love and prayers of those who shared our burden. Such a privilege is impossible to evaluate in terms of the strength it brings.

For our part, we never prayed for a miracle cure or that the medical prognosis would be proved wrong, only that Ciaran, with his mind alert and able to win at chess when he could no longer co-ordinate to move the men, would be spared distress and prolonged pain, and that with a power outwith ourselves to draw upon, we might have grace to rest in God's perfect will for us, however painful that might be.

'He who overcomes will inherit all these blessings and I will be his God and he will be my son' (Revelation 21:7).

2

DOUGLAS FRASER

I was born in 1945, the third of three brothers and the youngest by far. When I was still a tiny baby Mother suspected I could not see. She tested my sight, trying to make my eyes follow tapers and lights, but this just confirmed her in the belief that something was far wrong. So when I went into hospital for tests it was Mother who told the doctors that I was blind. I don't think that is unusual, defective eyesight is often first suspected by mothers caring for their little ones.

One doctor advised Mother that I should go to the Royal Blind School at Craigmillar in Edinburgh and, although others gave the opposite advice, she took me to Craigmillar where I became a pupil. I was not quite two years of age and was to remain there for the next sixteen years.

To School - aged two
As a toddler I found myself in the nursery department and enjoyed a very happy time there. But at five we moved into the 'big school' and that was hard. Pupils were aged between five and eighteen, and there seemed to be so many of them. I felt very lost as a new little boy there. It was vast compared with the cosy environment of the nursery.

Along with the change of school came a change of place to live as the nursery children and the school pupils were quite separate. My term time residence was with other children of my age in a building in the school grounds, while older boys and girls were in separate hostels, most of them within a short distance of the school. I think the transition must have been very traumatic, for my father recalls me changing from a happy little chap in nursery - always laughing and singing when on my visits home - to a much less carefree schoolboy. Even as a wee fellow I spent a lot of time on my own. I did have friends but did not always seem to fit in. Although I was not alone in finding school life hard, I did feel lonely.

But it was not all gloomy. In Craigmillar I became a member, first of the Wolf Cubs, then of the Boy Scouts. I enjoyed that, and can even remember my first meeting. It was a bit of a beanfeast and great fun! Every year I went camping with the Scouts.

I don't think blindness itself made me feel different; after all, from the age of two I lived in an environment in which blindness was normal and natural. But on my visits home I was aware I was not the same as the other children because they did not play with me as spontaneously as they did with each other. Perhaps part of the reason was that I was away at school most of the time and they did not know me very well.

Life in a boarding school is not the same as attending school and living at home. The days are fuller and organised. They have to be to keep children occupied and out of mischief! Sport was not my thing although I do remember playing football in the winters and cricket in the summers. Apart from that my sporting activities were confined to switching on the radio and listening to sports reports.

When I first went to school I did not get home at weekends but my parents sometimes came separately to visit me. When Mother came, on a Saturday about a month after the beginning of each term, we went into town to the shops and she told me what she saw there. Dad always chose a Sunday to visit and he and I went for long walks together, often finishing at the Meadows where I could play on the swings. Just before we returned to the school he took me to a sweet shop where he read me the names of all the sweets he could see in the window. As often as not I forgot what I wanted by the time I got inside and he had to read them to me all over again. He was not best pleased!

Later I was able to go home for occasional weekends. Some of the lads who went home more often took me with them from time to time. I liked that and had grand fun with them and their parents. Travelling had to be well organised. Older boys and girls were responsible for younger ones on the journeys which were made by service bus. On my very first week-end visit home I was accompanied by an older boy and met by my brother. The two of them liked each other a lot, and I remember feeling very pleased about that.

The three R's Craigmillar style

Our school curriculum was based on the '3 R's' - 'reading, 'riting and 'rithmetic'. Traditionally physiotherapy was a career blind folk pursued and those who intended doing so studied sciences. More able children learned French and Latin. My favourite subject was Braille because it opened up the world of books to me. To this day I am an avid reader.

It took me about two years to learn Braille. I had no knowledge of ink print although I knew that was what sighted people read and wrote. At school even those children who were partially sighted were not taught to use a pen or pencil. Learning Braille involved using a hand frame which was a board with a clamp keeping the paper in position. A guide went under the paper and another one on top. After each line the guide was slipped down to enable the next line to be written. We learned to write Braille in the opposite way to reading it - from right to left. This created problems for adult learners as it was different from what they had been used to. New types of machine have made that easier now. We used a style to make pricks on the underside of the paper and they could be felt and read when the sheet was turned over. This positioned the print for reading from left to right.

Years later a machine called the Stainsby made writing Braille much easier. It has three buttons on the right and three on the left hand side and a moving carriage. All the letters of the alphabet are made up of a combination of the dots these buttons make. For those learning Braille the first ten letters are the most difficult to understand, but after that the code begins to take shape because 'k' is an 'a' with a bottom dot, 'l' is a 'b' with a bottom dot and so on. 'W' breaks the code because Louis Braille who devised it was French and there is no 'w' in the French alphabet. A 'w' symbol had to be made up and added for users of English Braille.

For many years now I have used a Perkin's Brailler which is similar to an ordinary typewriter. My machine is well used for Torch Fellowship business. But more of that anon, the Torch Fellowship belongs later in my story!

Learning arithmetic was also very different for a blind child when I was at school. We used a Taylor frame, the top section of which had round holes which held metal pegs. The figures were made by turning the pegs. When it was at one angle it made the number one, turned round and fitted back into the hole made a two, turned at another angle made a three and so on up to eight. A nine required the peg to be removed, turned over and put at the one position. But that way up it had two points on it so the difference could be felt. From nine upwards numbers were built up in the normal way.

First steps in the Christian faith

Royal Blind School pupils who did not go home at weekends attended Sunday School in the church next door. There we met sighted children and learned with them. My belief in God was childlike. I knew right from wrong but thought the word 'sin' only applied to what I did, not to what I thought. So I tried to be good, but my mind still thought bad thoughts without me realising that they were just as sinful as evil words and actions.

Having gone to church and Sunday School all my school days I attended the Salvation Army with my mother when I went home aged 18. Because the hall was not full the band music echoed and I did not like that one little bit. Perhaps people with visual problems are more aware of sound distortion as we concentrate so hard on sounds.

An open air meeting followed the evening service and one night a young lady from the citadel invited me back after it to the youth fellowship. That led on to her arranging to call for me the following week to go to a carol service together. Although I liked the sound of her voice I forgot about the service! Perhaps that was the devil trying to prevent me going because something happened that night which changed my life.

When the officer leading the meeting closed it he prayed for those who were walking on the road to hell without realising their destination. I seemed to hear a voice inside me telling me that it was time I committed myself to being one of God's people. Before the meeting ended I accepted the invitation to go to the front where someone counselled me regarding my first real steps in the Christian faith.

Dogs: fellow workers and friends
While still at school I had applied for a guide dog then put the thought out of my mind. In the spring of the year following my conversion I learned that there was a dog

ready for me. Strangely I was not very keen to have one at first. I was so busy being a Christian that a dog seemed a complication I could do without. But I prayed about it and was led to accept the offer.

The training of guide dogs is the responsibility of the Guide Dogs for the Blind Association. Dogs are bred at the Association's breeding centre, then sent to puppy walkers who keep them as pets for a year. By then they are accustomed to people, different environments and forms of transport. Any problems are ironed out by a Supervisor from the Puppy Unit at the Training Centre who makes monthly visits.

The dogs then have harness training during which they are taught all the necessary movements. Their last few weeks of training take place at a centre in Forfar with their masters or mistresses who also have lots to learn. After going home they and their dogs continue learning together. Sometimes it takes as long as a year for a dog and owner to become a team though it often happens more quickly.

My first dog was called Jet because he was black, and I got him when he was two years old. We went everywhere together and he gave me a new kind of confidence. Sadly his sight began to fail after 9 years and he was retired. In 1976 I trained for another dog, Penny. She was smaller than Jet and we had many good times and doggy frolics. Penny and I worked well for another nine years.

My next dog, Glen, was again black. I got him in 1985 and sadly he had to be put down in 1993. He was a good

dog too, though it took me a long time to get used to him
for he was more sensitive than I first realised. Personality is important as a blind person and guide dog have
to work as a team. One memorable example of this
happened with Glen. We were out in long grass for
Glen's benefit and he was behind me. Suddenly he
marched past me, guiding me safely between two trees
which grew so closely together that I should certainly
have collided with one of them had he not taken over.
On another occasion I was about to cross the road when
he stopped me just as I heard the sound of a car whizzing
past. Had it not been for my dog I would have been under
it.

I now have Sandy who, at the time of writing, is just
eighteen months old. He is a great wee worker and very
fast.

The Torch Trust

Jet's arrival gave me a new kind of independence and
opened the door which led to my marriage. I was invited
to attend a branch of the Torch Fellowship - a Christian
organisation for visually impaired people - and it was
there I met Cathie, a sighted helper, who became my
wife.

There was one Torch Fellowship Group for the whole
of Glasgow and it met monthly in the city centre. After
we married Cathie and I realised that there was scope for
one in the west of the city. Much prayer went into
planning the Knightswood Torch Fellowship and, in
order not to take people away from the original group,

we met at a different time. Since then a third group has opened in the Partick area of the city and there is another one south of the River Clyde. Yet we are still reaching only a very small proportion of the hundreds of blind people in the area.

Although the Torch Trust aims to bring the gospel to blind people who do not attend church, most people who go are Christians, for the same problems exist in witnessing to blind as sighted people. It is difficult to generate interest in a meeting in someone who would rather be listening to sport. While we enjoy the fellowship of being believers together we try not to forget that our aim is to reach out with the gospel.

Because singing at meetings poses a problem for those of our members who are unable to read Braille or giant print, someone reads each verse of the hymns aloud before we sing it. Praise lasts a little longer than usual but everyone can then join in. We often have a singer and someone comes to speak. Guests are asked to talk for only 15 minutes because it is difficult for blind people to concentrate for much longer for they are unable to see the speaker. It is easy to nod off as anyone knows who has ever tried to listen to a sermon with his eyes shut!

Another branch of the ministry of Torch Trust is the preparation of tapes of Christian books: bio-graphy, autobiography, doctrine, missionary books etc. There is also a Braille library. Many blind people like me derive vast satisfaction from reading Christian books in Braille. Recent Trust projects include the preparation of books in a number of Indian and African languages, as well as a translation, bit by bit, of the New International Version of the Bible in Russian. It is being done in English Braille too. Hymn books are produced in both Braille and giant print. Giant print is bigger than conventional large print and not so readily available. I am chairman of my local branch and Cathie is secretary. She also organises transport for those who cannot travel alone.

Cathie and I are also active members of Partick Free Church in Glasgow and over the years our involvement has deepened. As a deacon one of my duties is to visit church members. I have nineteen people on my list and my dog is my invaluable companion on my visits. In one home there is a cat which has to be removed before I can go in. The ladies get a visit from their deacon but their cat does not!

Singing a joyful song
For the last fourteen years, when commitments to Torch Trust have allowed, I have been a member of the Glasgow Psalm Singers. Cathie has been going for longer. We have an annual recital and recently made a tape for the use of the young people of our church who have the opportunity to learn psalm singing for public worship. Any who choose to can sit a test on the subject and the tape was made to be of help to those who do.

I am a tenor and learning to sing the tenor part presents a challenge. Cathie gets the music in ink print and records my part by singing the tenor line in solfa on to a tape. Although I do not remember the names of the notes I do remember the melody and am able to learn my part from that. I practise it until I know it so well that I can concentrate wholly on reading the words - in Braille of course, and I prepare this beforehand. I also have an electronic keyboard on which Cathie sometimes plays my part for me.

Our church sings psalms rather than hymns. My psalm book is in three volumes and I have a further volume of paraphrases. The Bible I use is an Authorised Version in Braille and it takes up five feet of shelving. The beauty of my edition is that with each book of the Bible there is a list of the contractions and abbreviations used. Anyone who was not wholly familiar with Braille would find that of great benefit.

Using a white cane

The most obvious sign of blindness is the use of a white cane. I realised I would have to carry a cane when, as quite a young man, I was nearly hit by a car. Just last year when I was between dogs I learned long cane technique. One of the benefits of this is that you walk, as you do with a guide dog, in the middle of the pavement. The technique is different from an ordinary white cane which is used by tapping along the inside of the pavement. With the long cane you make an arc movement, tapping the cane at both ends of the arc. As you tap to the right you step forward with your left foot and vice versa. On approaching a road the movement changes slightly into a scanning motion; so instead of tapping you use the cane in a brush-like way thus anticipating uneven ground or obstacles. After remounting the pavement you return to the arcing movement.

I feel comfortable with a long cane, its only limitation being that the concentration involved is tiring and reduces the amount of walking I can do. This is not the case when working with a well-trained dog when the concentration is shared.

Work

After leaving school I waited just over a year before starting work in the Royal Workshops for the Blind (now known as Blindcraft), and I have been employed there ever since. This is a real factory with no perks other than that Guide Dogs for the Blind Association built a unit specially for the use of dogs and their owners. My first job was making mats of coconut fibre, mainly the kind that are used at house and shop doors but occasionally we made large gym mats. Then I made brushes, ones in which bristles are drawn through by wire. They are used for shoe cleaning or as pond brushes or deck scrubbers.

I am aware of the Lord helping me in even the simplest of ways. For example if I drop something I can almost hear a voice guiding me to where it is. Some would call this sixth sense but as God made all our senses I believe he has given me this very practical gift to help me live with my blindness.

My day begins about 5.30 am. I have always been an early riser. We had to be at school and I have never lost the habit. I catch my bus about 6.45 am, then get a special bus half an hour later which takes me right inside the factory gate. I put Sandy in the kennel and have a cup of tea before starting work at 8 am. There is a short break at ten, then I lunch and let Sandy have a run at 12.30 pm. My working day ends at 4.30 pm.

My present job in the factory is a mixture of bits and pieces all involved with bed making: putting sockets on the castors on bed legs, putting T nuts in bars, wrapping bed legs, and making up packs of fittings. Many Blindcraft beds are made on a contract basis for hospitals.

Looking forward

I live an ordinary kind of life, working Monday to Friday and involved in Christian activities some evenings and at week-ends. But the two cannot be separated, I am no less a Christian at work than in church or at a Torch Fellowship meeting. My blindness has become not so much a disability as a door of opportunity for which I am grateful to God whom I look forward to seeing in all his beauty in heaven.

3

PETER AND TIM MAIDEN

Tim begins his story

During my teenage years the annual extended summer holidays were all about cramming in as much activity as possible and getting far away from anything remotely resembling work.

Living very close to the English Lake District my friends and I would spend day after day swimming in rivers and lakes, boating, walking and camping. My memories of this time are of almost feverish activity: visiting unknown places, finding new swimming sites and trying ever more sports and activities.

I first became ill with what was later discovered to be Crohn's disease right at the beginning of summer 1987 and I can remember my biggest concern not being the long term consequences of the illness but rather the fact that I should miss out on all the summer fun.

Tim's father, Peter, looks back

My greatest concern for my three children, Becky, Tim and Dan, as they were growing up, was for their physical safety. I enjoyed my children - the terrible twos and the terrifying teens did not materialise. Spiritually they were showing the first signs of progress, but this frenetic activity? Travelling with young friends in cars, swimming in lakes and rivers, all the sport they could participate in encouraged me to commit them to the Lord many times a day.

Tim describes how his problems began
Life was incredibly easy for me as a child. To say my home life was comfortable and secure would be an understatement. Also I remember bragging about my almost total lack of health problems. So it came as quite a shock when, aged fifteen, a very sore and hugely swollen leg was diagnosed as a blood clot and I had to spend two weeks in hospital. The doctors assumed it was to do with a broken wrist, a simple footballing injury from a few weeks earlier.

Hospital was a depressing place: up at six, pills at seven, breakfast at eight, lunch at one, dinner at five-thirty and not a lot in between. At least a visit to a hospital clinic for one of the many nasty tests meant a bit of a change of scenery! But as I am a fairly pragmatic person I tried to make the best of it and I must say enjoyed all the attention I got. When I was finally allowed home I thought that was that and, apart from a few pills and a restricted left leg, I carried on with my life.

Being a Christian, I guess I should have gleaned some important spiritual lessons from this experience, but my faith at that point was probably 90% in my head. I knew God was with me and just got on with life without really questioning it all or worrying too much. God really had to shake me up properly to get my attention.

In 1988, whilst on a sailing trip in Scotland with my

church youth group, I developed severe stomach pains.
For the rest of the summer break I tried desperately hard
to carry on with my usual activities, but all the time felt
worse and worse. By the end of the holidays I was
doubled up in pain regularly, could not eat, and spent
nearly all my days in bed (apart from rather frequent
visits to the toilet!). I had never experienced such pain
before. When it racked me I could neither move nor
speak. The well-intentioned questions, 'where does it
hurt?' and 'can I do anything?' just seemed to infuriate
me. Couldn't they see I was in too much pain to reply?
And, while I could not have got by without the love and
care of my family, when the pain was at its worst I just
wanted to be left alone.

I was admitted to hospital again and, after three
weeks of the most unpleasant and uncomfortable tests
and much speculation and uncertainty, I was diagnosed
as having Crohn's disease.

Peter takes up the story

I was at a conference in Holland when Tim took ill this
second time and it was quite a shock to learn the news.
The fact that I could not be with him immediately was
very stressful. To be miles away when your son is in
excruciating pain is, to say the least, difficult.

I got back as quickly as public transport would allow.
What was wrong with Tim? Early tests were inconclusive. His weight loss had become alarming and he was
clearly very sick. When the diagnosis came as Crohn's
disease it was a relief to learn that while the condition

was incurable it was containable.

My life as Associate International Director of Operation Mobilisation was a busy one and, along with a full programme of itinerant preaching, resulted in a very satisfying but quite demanding lifestyle. This had only been possible because of the stability of our home life. Now, really for the first time, there were uncertainties in that area. But God was in control and, I thought, with the right medication Tim's problem would settle down and normality would resume.

Tim describes what happened next

The following four years were difficult. Regular bouts of sickness and severe pain were kept in check most of the time with medication. Every now and then I was admitted to hospital for more intensive treatment. During these times I sometimes wondered about the future. What kind of future would it be if I could never rely on my health? Life would be so constrained. But life went on, and I continued to enjoy almost all my previous activities. I was frustrated at times but never depressed. I knew that there were people far worse off than I was and I had a very real, if quite shallow, belief that God was with me and he was in control.

Only God knows when I became a Christian. I remember praying a little prayer in the back of my dad's car when I was about six. My sister Becky and I used to travel with him when he preached at various meetings and that night, after hearing him preach, we asked Dad what he meant when he invited people to give their lives to God. He explained and, since it seemed straightforward enough, we asked if we too could become Christians. He led us both in a very simple prayer, saying sorry to God for all that we had done wrong and asking him to forgive us. My understanding of the prayer was minimal and I guess I did not really understand what being a Christian meant until many years later.

Throughout my childhood, usually when I was feeling a bit guilty about something, I prayed similar prayers. Sometimes, fearing that I was perhaps not a Christian at all, I would pray that same prayer again as a kind of insurance policy.

But I never allowed the God to whom I was praying to make any difference to my life. As I was the only person in my class at school who went to church I felt it would probably be easier if my fellow pupils did not know I did. And I certainly was not going to go around telling them I was a Christian.

As time passed I began to realise that being a 'Sundays only' Christian was not enough. If God had really done as much for me as I believed he had, he deserved more than one day a week and a token prayer now and again. So, aged 16, I began a whole new commitment to God and tried to make serving and obeying him my priorities.

This was no radical transformation by any means, but since then, with many lapses, I have been learning what it means to have a relationship with God, to know his presence and his love, to communicate with him through prayer and reading the Bible and to see him actively involved and interested in my life. Things which in the past had been no more than vague niceties to be talked about in church, began to be wonderful realities in my life.

It was during these bouts of illness that my faith was first put to the test. At times, when in severe pain, I questioned God. Why did I have to suffer? Did he really care?

In 1991, just after my eighteenth birthday, I was driving up to Scotland with my sister Becky to catch a ferry to the Isle of Arran. We were going on an outdoor pursuits weekend with a group from church and were excited at the prospect of canoeing, gorge-walking and no sleep. A couple of hours after leaving home however (after slightly over-indulging on chocolate), I began to get pain in my stomach. But this being quite a regular occurrence I was not at first overly concerned. When the pain intensified, making me unable to drive, Becky took over and we continued northwards whilst I writhed about in the passenger seat in pain. Stubbornly and stupidly I insisted on us carrying on. I staggered aboard the ferry that evening assuming that after an increase in medication I would be better by morning.

When we reached Arran I had to be carried off the boat and the rough, twisting car journey to the outdoor pursuits centre was quite horrific. At every little bump I tried to stifle a scream, not always successfully. Having assured all around that I would be fine in the morning, by 2am I was so completely rigid with pain that I had to be taken to the tiny island hospital. Later that morning

I was back on the ferry, this time in an ambulance, and after doctors on the mainland failed to get me stabilised their only option was to operate.

Peter remembers

The normality I had expected to return after Tim's second hospitalisation did not materialise. Four years of uncertainty followed - my first question every time I rang home, 'How's Tim?' Too often the answer brought a lump to my throat. I was struggling with a number of things - Tim's suffering and me so often miles away, and the increased pressure and loneliness that meant for my wife Win.

It all came to a head in one of the most tense weekends of my life. I knew that Tim was not 100% well when he left for Arran, but that was nothing unusual for he constantly made a magnificent attempt not to allow his illness to hold him back, and in that I supported him completely. Although later that day I heard how ill he had become it was still a shock to receive a telephone call the next morning saying that he had been taken by ambulance to an infirmary on the mainland. It was Saturday morning. I cancelled a weekend of preaching engagements before leaving with Win to drive to Kilmarnock. Arriving there we found Tim in great pain and the doctors who were trying to relieve it discussing surgery. We were glad they felt that should take place in Carlisle and were attempting to stabilise him for the journey.

Ringing home to check on Dan, our second son, we

learned that Becky had broken her arm at the same youth weekend! I drove south leaving Win to travel to Carlisle with Tim when he was ready for the journey. What was God doing? I had learned long before that times of pressure and difficulty were often the most fruitful in my life, but this was heavy.

Over the previous six months I had been preparing for a meeting of the General Council of OM. This is the final decision-making body of the mission and it had some crucial issues to debate. It was due to commence in Holland in a matter of hours with people flying there from all over the world. What was my responsibility? Where should I be, Holland or hospital? The question did not take long to answer. Of course I should be with Tim. And from that moment on I knew I could 'cast all my care' about the Council meetings on the Lord.

Tim tells us about that time
With the prospect of surgery my prayer life suddenly took off. Because I was warned that the operation could be complicated and that there was no guarantee of success my fearfulness and uncertainty caused me, for the first time during my illness, to spend much time crying out to God for help.

When the time for my operation came round God answered my prayers and the prayers of many relatives and friends by giving me inner assurances that he was in control. With trepidation I accepted that his plan for my life was, as I had read in the Bible, 'good' and 'perfect' (Romans 12:2). The peace with which I went into theatre was not something I had 'drummed up' myself. It was an indescribable peace that came from knowing that despite years of giving God consideration only when it suited me, he loved me dearly and was with me whatever the outcome.

On waking up in intensive care I learned that the whole of the diseased part of my intestine had been removed without any complications arising. I remember bursting into tears, overwhelmed by God's goodness.

One unforgettable evening whilst recovering from the operation I took an adverse reaction to a particular anti-sickness drug and ended up convulsing for 24 hours. I was unable to control my body and struggled to breath. When doctor after doctor failed to come up with any explanation I thought I was going out of my mind. The convulsions were incessant and although the episode lasted only 24 hours it seemed like days. From the moment it started until the moment I came round after being given an antidote Dad was at my bedside. When I could not control my breathing he made me focus my eyes on his and forced me to copy his breathing pattern. At times, unable to breathe, I was filled with panic but Dad coaxed me through it all.

Despite this and other setbacks the operation was a success. I returned to normal life again slowly, having learned some valuable lessons. My experiences awakened me to love, both the earthly love of my family that I had always taken for granted and never fully appreciated, and the heavenly love of which I was beginning to catch glimpses but which I will never, in this life, fully comprehend.

Peter continues...

In Psalm 145:7 David writes: 'Men will bubble over with the memory of thine abundant goodness' (NASB margin). That is just how I feel when I look back over those tense days of operation and recovery. Through the many tears both of concern and joy there was always a deep assurance of an all-powerful God in sovereign control. There was also a wonderful sense of 'family'. At such times you realise what a magnificent family the family of God is. Calls assuring prayer came from immediate family, church family and the worldwide Christian family. One call from a church leader in California - a church I had never even heard of - stands out. The caller on the end of the line said, 'You don't know us but we have been praying for Tim. We know his situation. I am just on my way to the church prayer meeting and I want you to know we are with you.'

God also provided a very special friend as close to the action as could be! Stephen Alfred is a surgeon from India who spent a number of years in Britain. He had come to Carlisle not long before, joined our church and become our friend. The events of the next few hours were to deepen that friendship. Stephen was to assist the surgery. He sat with us in hospital until going into theatre and, immediately the operation was over, telephoned with the news of its successful outcome. I spent the three hours of Tim's surgery in his bedroom, crying out to God to use the skill he had given to the surgeons and to heal him. My joy mingled with tears on visiting Tim in the intensive care unit will never be forgotten. Joan, a Christian nursing friend from our church, was responsible for him. And in the after care ward, Clare, another believer who is now married to Stephen, was also involved in his care from time to time.

Tim was recovering well. Could he now look forward to freedom from pain? But during one visiting time Tim began to lose control of some of his muscles and breathing became difficult for him. For 24 hours no one seemed to know what to do. Four or five different specialists were marched in but all were confused. Though nurses and doctors were always close by, for many hours I was left alone with Tim. I had two prayers - God help him to breathe, and may this terrifying experience not leave its emotional mark on him. God brought him through and though he has had flashbacks to those terrible hours he has come through strong. Such is the abundant goodness of God!

Tim brings us up to date

The eighteen months following surgery was an incredible time for me. Completely free of pain, and feeling on top of the world again, I took a year out between school and university and, jetting out to South Africa, back-packed around for four months. I also spent some time there on an Operation Mobilisation training team. Being alone for much of the time and so far from home comforts, my relationship with God seemed to blossom.

In very difficult and at times scary situations I learned what it was really to trust God in all things.

This stood me in good stead for university life. It is said that the most stressful times of life are suffering bereavement in the family, moving house and going on holiday. Leaving home to start university is almost like those three rolled into one - with a total change of situation away from family and friends. And the pain began to recur. Managing to struggle through the first term, by my second I could no longer attend lectures and was vomiting regularly. Faith was stretched to its limit as I was convinced that God wanted me at university, in fact convinced that I was on exactly the right course. Having just begun to settle in properly, with work going well, it all ground to a halt. I could not continue.

I was confused, almost angry with God. Why get me to university and seem to confirm I was in the right place only to end it like this? I guess I had seen God at work too much in my life to doubt my faith totally, but the situation I found myself in brought great heart-searching and considerable anguish. I had become used to pain, had learned to cope with it, but spiritual struggling was another kind of pain altogether.

Returning home from university, virtually resigned to not going back for that year at least, I read James 5:14-15: 'Is one of you sick? He should call the elders of the church to pray over him and anoint him with oil in the name of the Lord. And the prayer offered in faith will make the sick person well; the Lord will raise him up.' I had read these verses many times before without really taking in what was written. As I had never heard of such a thing happening in my church, I had not given the possibility much thought. This time it was different and after two or three days praying about it I knew these verses applied to me. The situation was almost black and white. God wanted me at university and this illness was stopping me being there. I had to do what these verses told me and trust that God would heal me.

My rather conservative church elders, almost to my surprise, did come and pray for me along with their wives. There were no flashes in the sky or funny sensations, in fact there was nothing externally spectacular at all, just a simple loss of pain. I have now been free of health problems for almost eighteen months and am half way through my university course, itching to return to Africa to work there. As Crohn's disease can recur at any time the future is uncertain, but one thing I am sure of, the God of wonderful grace and miracles will see me through.

A last word from Peter

Today I see a young man, faith strengthened, love deepened through the experience he has described. I am part of a human family drawn even closer together and have a deeper appreciation than ever before of the family of God.

As I write this Tim has just left for Mongolia from where he will travel overland to Moscow and then Crackov before meeting up with me in Holland. It seems our children are determined to keep me on my knees!

4

PAULINE HILLIER

The words stabbed me. 'To think that any offspring of mine should believe that outdated superstition! You are no longer worthy to be my child.' Father went on digging the garden, turning over clods of earth and slicing the roots of the weeds before moving on. His words cut me sore but did not root out and kill the young shoot of faith that was growing in my heart.

What Father said that day in the garden had echoes of the past. I was nineteen and trying desperately to run our home, nurse Mother who was ill and sometimes violent towards me, and have a welcoming meal ready and a smile on for Dad coming in. But I wasn't coping. I had gone to my doctor for help and decided, as a result of being told by him that I was heading for a breakdown, that I would have to tell Dad all. I tried to explain to him what love and loyalty had kept inside me, but he did not understand. ' I have known for over a year how you ill-treat your mother,' he accused. 'You are unworthy to be our child! We came out here for your sake - IT IS ALL YOUR FAULT.'

These memories are still vivid half a century later, perhaps because they were dark lines cutting across an otherwise pleasant canvas. My father was right, they had gone to the country for my sake. They had done so much for my sake. They had loved me and I loved them dearly.

My family tree

My earliest memories are of beauty, for my mother loved beautiful things. She was not a cuddly mum but I recall once sitting on her knee tracing Jack Frost's pictures on the window and being enchanted by them. From the age of two I lived in Bristol where I remember being taken across the Clifton Suspension Bridge in my pushchair. What could be more exciting for a little girl than that, to see from such a great height the world in miniature below?

Mother was brought up with beautiful things but had cut herself off from many of them by marrying Father. Love for him made her leave behind the twelve-bedroomed mansion which had been her home, and the cook, housemaid, parlourmaid and chauffeur. Following her marriage she and her parents had little left in common. Father's background was a foreign world to them. He was the son of a handyman and grave digger, and motherless from the age of eleven. But there was worse to come. Dad did not believe in God and inside him a fire of hatred and contempt burned against religion in any shape or form. He was true to his conviction to the end, his will containing specific instructions for an atheist funeral.

But Mother loved him and I was the child of their love. I can close my eyes and picture myself, a frail and rather lonely little girl playing in the garden of our council house. I did not go to school because of ill health and spent part of each day lying on a little canvas stretcher Dad made for me to try to correct the curvature of my spine. This sounds a trial, but to lie in the garden on a summer day surrounded by marigolds and lupins, pinks, cornflowers and roses, to me that was bliss. A little girl lived next door and from time to time we talked through the hedge. But as Eileen went to Sunday School we were not allowed to be friends.

Schooling - my way

One occasional playmate passed sentence, 'Thee'll be the daftest kid in all Clapton if thee don't go to school!' Little did he know. The *Children's Encyclopaedia* must have been well worn by the time I outgrew its use. My education centred on it and on the radio, a crystal set with a cat's whisker and headphones. I followed radio lessons on a wide variety of subjects and completed the set work which went along with them.

To my delight I was able to go to school for half days during two terms when I was ten. I loved it so much and how sad I was when I became too unwell to continue and had to leave behind all but the memories of laughter and games, of teasing the teacher and being kept in for being naughty. I confided my sadness in my notebook, 'My life has been very traggic - peeple do not unnerstand me.'

I am not quite sure what the spelling says about the standard of my education but the sentiment was not really a reflection of my life. I enjoyed simple pleasures: bread toasted at the fire and my nose toasted too, cherry cake for a treat, time spent in the garden with Dad, and illicit play through a hole in the hedge with Eileen. They were the stuff of childhood happiness and fond memories.

But my parents were too socially aware for me to think that everyone's world was full of cornflowers and pinks. I listened to them discussing the welfare state, poverty, free education, better housing, free milk and 'Utopia'. My father was working towards Utopia. It is easy to forget how things have changed in the years since my childhood. Hospitalisation then was a fearful prospect. I remember the columns in the local paper each night listing the condition of the children who were in the isolation hospital with scarlet fever, measles, mumps or diphtheria. No names were used. Each child was given a number and anxious parents scanned the lists of numbers under three headings, 'Improved', 'Stable' and 'Gravely Ill'.

A new home and a new life

Bristol is a beautiful city but, when I was a child, its beauty was often hidden in a thick fog. Our doctor suggested that my chronic chest condition would be helped by a move to the country. And so it was we found ourselves in a four-roomed bungalow on half an acre of land in a hamlet outside the city, and all on a mortgage of £250! And so it was also that years later my father was able to say, 'We came out here for your sake. It is all your fault.'

Life in the country started well. Mother and I picked mushrooms and blackberries, dandelion leaves and nettle tips. Father converted the builder's site into a lovely and productive garden. Milk came from the nearby farm, and eggs from our own chickens. Father's Trade Union activities took him to conferences and because he was on the Executive Committee Mother and I went too and stayed in smart hotels.

Each year I got a new evening dress which covered my surgical boots and made me feel really grand. It was during one such conference that Mother and I were taken with other wives and children to visit Buckfast Abbey. In the souvenir shop a monk handed me my purchase, made the sign of the cross, and wished me God's blessing. 'If there is a God,' I remember thinking, 'he must be nice.'

Gathering storm clouds

Life was fun and full but clouds were coming over the horizon. Dad's involvement with the Trade Union Movement took more and more time and eventually became all-consuming. Mother had no friends for the local activities centred round the church. They had moved to the country for my sake, hadn't they? With this my mother would taunt me. And over the next six years I watched as my mother's complaints became anger then despair, and as her behaviour grew disturbed and violent.

We moved to the country when I was eleven and it seemed a dream come true. But as my health improved Mother's deteriorated and within four years I was nursing her and running our home. By the time I was nineteen our dream had become a nightmare and it is only by God's grace I can tell without bitterness of occasions when Mother lunged at me with a knife, or caught me by the ears and repeatedly crashed my head against a wall. But no one else knew. My father was working all the hours of the day and night for the great ideal of Utopia, and I felt that by covering up for Mum I was helping him get there.

But I could not keep it up and when my doctor warned me that I was heading for a breakdown I told Dad what I had in love withheld from him, believing he would understand. My hero betrayed me. After reading the doctor's letter Father tore it up and threw it in the fire. 'Some doctors will say anything if you pay them enough,' was his only response. Mother's violence frightened me, but Father's anger cut through all the layers of love I had for him. 'I have known for over a year how you ill-treat your mother. You are unworthy to be our child!' But even as my father failed me my heavenly Father began to draw me to himself.

Into my life at this time of great isolation came a friend. When Father told me that he had volunteered to take a little girl as an unofficial evacuee I was furious. My hands were already full and in any case there was nowhere for the child to sleep - apart from my bed. I did not look forward to Ann coming, although I suppose I welcomed her well enough. But before very long had passed the child was the friend I had never had. She was nine and I twenty, over fifty years later we are still dear friends.

The end of the road

Life had seemed so worthless that I had even tried to commit suicide, though my first effort says more about my imagination than technical expertise or common sense. I rigged up a home-made guillotine using a scythe, some string and a nail on the wall. A headache was the only result, and the head and the ache remained firmly attached to the rest of me.

It was Ann who prevented me trying again. I had it planned. Next time there was a thunderstorm I would lean against a pylon in the hope that it would be hit by lightning and I would die, as a cow had done not long before. But when the next rumble of thunder came, Ann was in my bed and I would have had to climb over her to go out the window. On seeing the child lying asleep I could go no further. She needed me and I needed her. God used our unwelcome evacuee to save my life.

But Ann was not the only new friend I made. God had two more planned. Marie came to our village as a member of the Women's Land Army and she and I met accidentally, then by arrangement each day when I went for milk. We both played the violin and found that we had other interests in common. As Father was in the Home Guard and often away overnight, Marie came to help me care for Mother and Ann. So we were able to build a friendship for which I have often thanked God.

About this time a new vicar, Rev Charles Forrester (Boss), arrived on the scene. Unlike his predecessor he had not been warned about Father's hatred of all things Christian and he arrived totally unsuspecting at the door.

As Mother was asleep, Ann at school, and Father in town, I had at last an opportunity to question someone who might know how to tell me about God. But I had to take precautions. I hid Mother's clothes so she could not come upon us talking and send Boss away!

Surely Boss was taken by surprise. 'You must tell me whether or not there is a God, because, if there is not, I don't wish to go on living,' was my opening gambit. He answered my questions. I poured out my desperation. He visited, supported and strengthened when I needed it most. Why, you might ask, did Mother allow this to happen? I can only think that she was remembering her childhood days in a churchgoing home, and that as she and my father grew further apart, his hatred of religion had less effect on her.

Boss encouraged me to pray and I did so daily in the words of the man who fell at Jesus' feet, 'Lord, I believe. Help my unbelief.' For seven months I prayed that prayer. God listened and prepared a big surprise for me. On Ann's birthday I climbed into the attic to hunt for a Punch and Judy I had had as a child. I did not find it, but I did find a Bible. In our atheistic home, where religion was hated, I found a Bible. It must have been a baby gift to me because it had my name written on it.

A wonderful new beginning
In the middle of that night, by the light of a candle so as not to wake Ann, I read Mark's Gospel and life took on meaning. I pictured the soldiers hammering nails through Jesus' hands and I looked at my own. That day Mother

had chased me and attacked me with a screwdriver and I had a deep wound on my wrist. Suddenly I knew that Jesus' wounds were as real as mine and that he was alive and could be my friend. By the time I lay down on my mattress on the floor I was born again into the great family of Jesus Christ.

Some people give the impression that when you become a Christian the world is a garden of roses. My rose garden was full of thorns. Because, like my father, I could not tolerate hypocrisy, I soon told him I had become a Christian believer. It was that which provoked his stinging comment with which this account began.

Boss knew my situation because I had told him about it. But he had also seen it for himself as he called unexpectedly one day when Mother was in the act of attacking me. He sent for Father who listened to what the vicar had to say. Father said his piece too: they had made enormous sacrifices for me and he loved me although he did not wear his heart on his sleeve. But on the way home his verdict on the interview was this, 'So you've got the vicar in your pay as well.'

Wars within and without

Aged twenty one, and after six years of caring for my mother, I began to suffer symptoms of severe stress: spells of shaking, vomiting, nightmares and unsightly patches of eczema on my face each time Mother was violent. After much thought, prayer and discussion with Boss and Marie, I gave Father six months notice that I was leaving home. In those war-time days there were plenty of women past call-up age who could look after Mother and free me for war service. I had hoped that giving Father notice would encourage him to take over responsibility for Mother, but he did nothing. So six months later Marie and I left the bungalow behind us and walked the two miles to the railway station on the first stage of my journey to join the Women's Land Army. God so arranged it that we were given a double posting, a very unusual event, for my Father in heaven knew I needed her.

For some time I had been troubled with nightmares, and guilt at leaving Mother caused me to begin to hallucinate. During the nights I saw skeletons moving around the room. Marie offered practical help and love. She sat in the dark holding a toasting fork and each time I hallucinated showed me the fork and reassured me, 'You just tell me when you see them, and I'll jab 'em!' She could have told me it was all in my mind, but she didn't. She might have been afraid of my strange fears, but she wasn't. Marie could have told me to pull myself together, but she didn't. She loved me through it all.

My friend was patient with my nightmares too. The dream was always the same: I was digging and my spade hit a coffin on which the words 'Grace May Hillier' were inscribed. The lid flew open to expose the skeleton of my mother and I would be struck by fear as it leapt up and dragged me in. Little wonder that I woke up screaming.

In 1943 God enabled me to overcome that fear. Marie and I were sharing a billet and one summer day we set out to Cheddar to pick strawberries to make jam for our larder. After a lovely but wearying time we went to the local cafe, The Cave Man, for tea. As all of Cheddar seemed to have arrived there before us, the waitress directed us through a narrow passage to another room where there was still some space.

Peace ... be still

There in the passage I froze with fear. Directly ahead of me was a life-size copy of a prehistoric skeleton and I had no alternative but pass it. Marie was afraid too, afraid for me. She, who had supported me for so long, thought this might tip me over the brink into insanity. But God used it to do quite the opposite. It was as though he told me, in that terrifying moment, to look long and hard at the thing I feared most. I did. He gave me the strength to look at the hideous thing, its dark eye-sockets and grinning jaw. I looked. I stared. And slowly, so slowly, my arm was guided forward by my loving heavenly Father till I held the skeletal fingers in my clammy hand.

I was twenty-two then, I am seventy-three now, and I have never dreamed that dream again. Nor have I hallucinated since.

The ripples reach out

There is so much said and written today about child abuse and there are many wounded people as a result of the kind of physical and emotional cruelty I knew in my teen years. It is a subject which Christians have difficulty sharing because they, of all people, are loyal to their families and want to spare those close to them any hurt, even those who have hurt them. I was loyal when I needed to be but the need for silence has passed.

Without Christ I might well have become another statistic - just one more victim of abuse, carrying on the cycle of abuse with which we have sadly become so familiar. But that did not happen because Jesus took hold of me and helped me take hold of my fears as surely as he helped me grasp that bony hand. Instead of becoming part of a self-perpetuating cycle of abuse, I have spent my adult life telling about the goodness of God and seeing people come to faith through the ministry I have been given. God broke the cycle. And as the pain of rejection abated I discovered that he had enabled me never to stop loving my father and my mother.

I would not have chosen my teenage years to be as they were, but I am grateful that God used that time to make himself real to me and to change my life completely. First he healed my mental illness and emotional hurt. Later he showed me the darkness in my own heart, the darkness of resentment and lack of forgiveness. And later still God called me into full-time service of which I will tell you just a tiny bit.

From 1948 until 1950 I trained as a Church of England Parish Worker, then found myself in the slums of Birmingham working with the poor but wonderful people there. From Birmingham I went to Dover, then to a large country parish in Cornwall. After Cornwall came Dagenham, where part of my time was spent with drug addicts. My career changed direction then and I was led to work for a time in a Christian Conference centre in Ireland. Having taken me out of England the Lord gave me quite a surprise by calling me to Singapore. I served in Singapore Cathedral and seemed well suited to the job - after all, what the church there had asked for was 'an oldish, unshockable woman!' After seven years I was invalided home and have worked in Bristol ever since.

Mental, emotional, spiritual, physical - God, the Great Healer, has wrapped me in his arms of love all my life. How I love to sing John Newton's hymn:

Jesus, my Shepherd, Saviour, Friend,
my Prophet, Priest and King -
My Lord, my Life, my Way, my End,
accept the praise I bring.

Like my father I have left instructions for my funeral. Those who attend will sing:

Happy, if with my latest breath
I may but gasp His name,
Preach Him to all and cry in death,
'Behold the Lamb!'

5

ALAN AND ANNE FRASER

Anne tells Lourdes' story

'Do you know what Lourdes did when you were upstairs, Senora?' asked Consuelo. 'She was so hungry that she ate the food from the cat's plate.' We hardly knew Lourdes then, but we grew to know and love her.

As missionaries in Lima, Peru, involved in education and church work among people for whom life was hard but not desperate, we were conscious we lacked daily contact with the abject poverty in the shanty towns that ringed the city. It was our prayer that somehow we would have a channel through which we could help a little.

One day as Alancito, our three-year-old son, watered the grass outside our gate I heard a woman talking to him. When I spoke to her she asked about our family and told me about hers. As her husband had more or less abandoned her, she went to work carrying the baby with her and leaving the other children locked in their straw matting hovel. She asked if I had any old clothes I could spare for her children. Unfortunately just the day before I had sent out-grown clothes to the girls' school as part of a project they were doing in aid of the needy. It was difficult to tell her we had none.

For the next few days I could not get that woman and

her children out of my mind. How could I have turned her away when we had so much and she so little?

When I saw her the following Saturday I gave her a small bag of clothes. On Monday she was at the door. My immediate reaction was, 'Not back for more already!' How wrong I was. 'I've just come to say thank you very much for the clothes, Senora. They all fitted beautifully,' said Lourdes. 'Could I sweep out your garage for you? I wish to thank you.' Although my natural caution asserted itself I agreed and gave her a sandwich which she ate ravenously. I asked her if she was given lunch where she worked. That was normal practice. She replied that she was but took it home to share with her children. She often arrived hungry after that but always insisted on doing something in return for a little food.

It was in these early days that the incident with the cat's food took place. Poor Lourdes was too hungry to wait for lunch. Looking back I am impressed by her honesty. She could easily have taken other food but she did not. How misplaced had been my suspicions. As our relationship grew I marvelled at the personal standards Lourdes had clung to throughout her difficult life.

Domestic help is necessary in that dusty atmosphere and hot, enervating climate. It also provides employment for those desperate to earn. As our home help was about to leave it seemed a good idea to offer Lourdes work. I did not know then how much I would come to need her.

Soon it became apparent that Lourdes was also

spiritually hungry. Hearing of Jesus' love awakened a desire to know more and she enthusiastically agreed to regular Bible studies. The Lord brought her to trust in him. But her problems did not go away. Lourdes' husband returned but treated her badly and neighbours gave her a hard time too. She became involved in the local evangelical church and before long a women's Bible study was held in her humble home. Our prayers had been answered in opening up this opportunity to help. But the Lord was also preparing answers to prayers that had not yet been uttered.

Lima: Alan introduces 'The City of the Kings'

Lima is a typical third world city. Its growth is rapid due to a high birth rate coupled with immigrants from the impoverished country areas drawn there by an elusive promise of employment, education and a brighter future for the next generation. This creates an explosive mixture of rich and poor. Threaded through the class mix is a blend of ancient and modern: gracious buildings from a bygone age with the best that modern architecture can create; shanty towns with their forest of TV aerials; ancient cars jostling for position on the crowded roads with the very latest models; and traditional costumes mingling with the ubiquitous jeans culture. To such a city Anne and I came as a young newly married couple in November 1973.

I worked as a teacher in Colegio San Andres. This boys' school with a high reputation for quality education at low cost was founded in 1917 by the Free Church of

Scotland as its first mission venture into Latin America. As my parents were deeply interested in overseas mission work, I was brought up surrounded by interesting people who worked in all parts of the globe.

My first contact with the school had been through the Rev James Macintosh who was head teacher. Later some former pupils came to share our home in Edinburgh for some months. Thus it was natural that I should think of Peru when considering my career. Was I not a member of the Free Church, a science graduate and about to enter Teacher Training College? Did not the Free Church have need of such in Lima? Did this constitute a divine call? For some it would not. For me it was sufficient. Anne and I agreed to share our lives wherever the Lord led and in due course were accepted as missionaries to serve in Peru.

We looked forward with excitement and trepidation to a distant country, a foreign language and a strange working environment.

By nature I was not adventurous and perhaps ill-equipped for life in a Latin culture. But with all our mixed motives, fears, character and spiritual deficiencies we set out on what we were convinced was the Lord's choice of route for us. Looking back now, with a clearer understanding of my own failings and inadequacies, I remain convinced that the right choice had been made.

Our first home was in a flat next to the school. It was not the latest in luxury but it was clean, comfortable and had electricity and running water. In those days, before a collapsed economy brought severe deficiencies in public health, we could even drink the tap water. Shopping was mostly done at the local supermarket which had much of what we needed even if the choice was very restricted. In the street markets delicious fruits we had never heard of before were cheaply and abundantly available. What public transport lacked in comfort (and safety!) it made up for in speed, frequency and cost. Modern clinics attended to our medical needs and a chemist could be found all round the clock. The jungle or the high Andes provided a diversity of interesting holiday venues. As the children grew they integrated happily into school, church and wider community, becoming bilingual and making friends with others from many different backgrounds.

A special child - by Anne

Donald came into this world on 28th October 1982 and we were soon home and being fussed over by the other three children, Margaret, Kirsty and Alancito. He was a good baby. He slept well, fed well and was not demanding. However, Don was slow to sit and crawl and by the age of two showed little inclination to walk. Seeds of doubt began to grow into concern. Initial tests proved inconclusive.

Don started physiotherapy just three months after Lourdes began working with us. It was very time consuming. Lourdes, who came each week-day morning, related well to all the family, particularly Don. Her inventiveness in a crisis and her capacity to find lost articles were especially helpful.

An Australian nurse recommended to Alan that Don be taken home to Scotland for further tests, not to put a label on his condition but to discover his potential and show us how best we could help him. When Alan suggested I go alone with the boys, an idea that held no appeal for me, I did not take him seriously. Soon afterwards delegates from the Free Church's Foreign Missions Board visited Peru and strongly supported the idea of Don going to Scotland for further tests. I had to face seriously the prospect of taking Don and Alancito to Edinburgh.

Alancito had broken his leg and was in plaster from his armpits to his toes on one side and to his knee on the other. Would he be fit to travel when the plaster was removed? I knew I would get lost in the maze of corridors at airports. I was not good at sleeping on aircraft and did not relish twenty four hours with the boys without sleep. Besides, Alan and I had never been separated before. I was on the verge of flatly refusing to go when a post card arrived from ladies in the Kingussie congregation sending greetings for 1986 and quoting Deuteronomy 31:8: 'The LORD, he it is that doth go before thee; he will be with thee, he will not fail thee, neither forsake thee: fear not, neither be dismayed' (AV). I realised I was not being asked to go in my own strength, that God supplies all our needs.

We travelled in January. As Alancito's plaster had been removed shortly before he was able to cope with the necessary walking. Lourdes was well established in the household and it eased my mind to know that she would cope with the cleaning and the washing and be on hand while Maggie, our eleven-year-old, attended to the cooking. The daunting task of dealing with doctors and hospital staff was eased by the care and loving concern shown by all at the Royal Hospital for Sick Children in Edinburgh. I also had the joy of being with my parents for six weeks and seeing other relatives too.

The verdict at the end of it all was that Don would be physically clumsy and severely mentally handicapped.

Looking back I am surprised how calmly we took the news. It was not a shattering experience. He was our wee boy, much loved by all the family, and the prognosis resulted more in a concern over how best to help him. In many ways the prospect of perhaps having to leave Peru and trying to work out whether this was what God really wanted us to do was far more difficult. We were supported by many of the Lord's people, some unknown to us, who took a loving and prayerful interest in us. For them we give thanks.

The speech therapist who showed me how to use the 'portage system' as a means of home education stressed the need for Don to be integrated into a totally English speaking play group. When I told her I doubted that such a thing existed in Lima, she said, 'Well start one.' Back in Lima I searched the city. Nothing doing. How could I organise one? I had no experience nor training in this field and where would I get six English-speaking children whose parents wanted such a play group? After much prayer and asking around, four of us with our four children got together to plan one. The three other mothers had all been teachers, one specialising in teaching handicapped children! On reading up about it we learned that four, not six as I had imagined, was the recommended number for two to three-year-olds.

Let me introduce you to the children. Danny was a two-and-a-half-year-old whose English mother, Liz, had come as a missionary and married a Peruvian pastor. Then there was Daniel who was the same age. His mother Gail, an Anglo American, was born and brought up in Peru and married to a Peruvian lawyer. They were both Christians. Adrianna, aged two, was the youngest and very bright. Her mother, Pam, from the USA, was married to a Peruvian diplomat. Don was three and a half years old. We met twice a week. The play group turned out to be a happy event for all, meeting the needs of more than Don. Our own house was the venue as it was most suitable. God's hand was in this provision. We had moved house two years earlier and of all the houses we had looked at none would have been as appropriate for the play group.

Following the diagnosis we had to give thought to Don's education and the following year was spent sussing out the provision made for children with special needs in that great city of seven million inhabitants. I still feel sad at much of what I saw. Dedicated, caring teachers and therapists lacked training in modern methods. But eventually it seemed I had found the right place. A well trained specialist took a class of six children, all with speech defects, (which was and is one of Don's greatest problems) and she had one space free. She offered a stimulating programme and was sympathetic and kind to us. 'I'm willing to take Donald,' she said, 'He can start tomorrow. I strongly advise that you forget about speaking English at home. This child has problems enough without coping with two languages.' Had she thrown cold water over me I would have been less shocked. I thought her's was the ideal place. How could we forget about English at home? It was the family language and important for the other children who spoke Spanish with friends, at church and school. It was then I began to consider seriously the possibility that we might have to leave Peru for Don's sake.

In March 1987 we were due to go on furlough but it now seemed possible we would be leaving for good. For Alan this was unthinkable. There had been no recruits from Scotland for some time and his plans for a new school building and his many educational projects were progressing in such a way that it seemed madness to quit at that point. What were we to do? We had been praying for guidance for more than a year and furlough was only three months away. In desperation I asked the Lord for an answer within a fortnight. His answer was beautiful. He gave me perfect peace. Suddenly I was quite content to leave the matter in his hands. He would show us in his own time what his will for us was. It was so good to know that the Lord not only heard my prayer but that he also cared for us.

Alan shares the pain of parting
Leaving Lima was one of the most difficult and lonely

things I have ever done. Indeed, because the decision that we should uproot ourselves from the work which had become so intertwined with our lives proved impossible for me to make, I left it to the Foreign Mission Board which had supported us for fifteen years. They saw no other option open to us. We had been given a special child. Some of his basic needs required us to return to Scotland. Leaving Peru was unavoidable.

Even five years on the pain of that parting remains a potent force in my life. A sense of failure dominated and uncovered events and areas of my life that I would have preferred to forget. Flashbacks came at unexpected moments and with no apparent reason or prompting. Life's sense of purpose clouded and I felt I understood Elijah when he asked that he be allowed to leave this world. I was no different from many others who have returned from what they considered to be their life's work to an uncertain future. One Christian psychologist has drawn a parallel between this situation and a bereavement.

It is not that there had been no successes. There were things which I would not change if given the opportunity to do them again, even though some caused controversy. In other areas I wish I could turn the clock back. How good to know that our acceptance by our heavenly Master is all of grace. Even the faithful servant must say, 'I am but an unprofitable servant.' For the rest of us there is the knowledge that our failures are covered by the blood of the Lamb.

But the Lord did not leave me with doctrine alone as

comfort. Encouragement, especially from former colleagues and parents of pupils, came when I needed it. The granting of land by the government for a new school building was a great boost to morale and a positive note on which to bow out. Why then the sense of compulsory redundancy? To answer that would take more space than we have here, more patience than I have the right to expect of any reader, and an objectivity of which I am not yet capable. But one thing I know. My involvement in the work had become like that of a playwright creating a great work of art. I had written myself into the script in too permanent a manner. Perhaps I had become engrossed in the work as an end in itself. But when God apportions blame I know he will declare my sentence fully paid by Jesus Christ, who gave himself for me and who has never left me and never will.

I agreed with the Foreign Board of the Free Church to remain in Peru for eighteen months to allow for a period of transition. Anne and the children would spend that time in Edinburgh and I would have a number of visits home, each lasting several weeks.

Home alone - Anne takes up the story
The first few months in Scotland were traumatic for me. Like Peter I concentrated on the waves around me rather than on the Lord. The New Year's Day service of 1988 changed that. Rev A G Ross, then minister of Free Buccleuch and Greyfriars, spoke of how God did not promise to remove sharp stones and boulders from our path but to give us the footwear to walk over them. I felt

he was speaking to me alone and I was reminded again of the words of Deuteronomy 31:8:

> 'The LORD himself goes before you and will be with you; he will never leave you nor forsake you. Do not be afraid; do not be discouraged.'

How many times I have had to learn that lesson.

Once I accepted our situation I was able to get things in perspective. Looking back to that time, the traumatic moments are fading and blessings becoming more clear. After all the years in Peru we were able to enjoy the wider family circle. This was particularly important for the children. Both Alan's family and mine were very supportive. During that time a closer bond was forged between myself and my mother, the memory of which I cherish now that she is no longer with us. My sister Cora's sympathetic ear and common sense kept me going. Contact with students and others in the congregation and in Don's nursery school was enriching.

During Alan's visits home we spent all the time we could together and have memories of precious moments, of walks, trips to places of interest and local coffee shops. These were invaluable times of strengthening the bonds that were under more of a strain than ever before.

Alan also visited congregations in various parts of the country to talk about the work in Peru. He always enquired about special education facilities. There was no point in coming back for Don's benefit and settling where adequate facilities were unavailable for him.

When the opportunity of an interview came it was where we had least expected it. But not only was a job available in Stornoway, in the island of Lewis, but also a place in the very well equipped special unit in the primary school where Don was quickly accepted in an atmosphere of Christian love.

One of the psalms I love to sing is one which I earnestly prayed whilst singing as a teenager at a Youth Conference. It was when I realised that things were not right between myself and my God.

> Lo, I do stretch my hands
> To thee, my help alone;
> For thou well understands
> All my complaint and moan:
> My thirsting soul desires,
> And longeth after thee,
> As thirsty ground requires
> With rain refresh'd to be.

Psalm 143:6
(Metrical Psalms)

That is still our prayer today.

A last word from Alan

The way in which employment and a house became ours reminded us that God had not abandoned us. We are now surrounded by a praying community and enjoy the privilege of frequently working with those who love the Lord. The church community we have become part of is familiar to us as we had both been brought up in the

Free Church in the Highlands of Scotland. In some respects it is different, reflecting a vibrant local tradition and close personal contact on the part of many with times of spiritual revival. Consequently there is an emphasis on a deep personal experience of God's favour and a cultivation of inner holiness. Although I was slow to admit it I needed that experience as part of the healing process.

6

IAN YULE

I came into the world twenty minutes earlier than my twin brother on 6th January 1957. We grew up in a good home in Bearsden, near Glasgow, being educated first at Bearsden Primary School then at Bearsden Academy. When we were little my parents put my brother and me in Sunday School at a local church, but we soon rebelled against it. I have memories of sticking pieces of paper into the hammer of my father's alarm clock so that he wouldn't hear it when it went off on a Sunday morning! The family ceased to have any church connection before I left primary school.

In 1974, as my final year in school ended, I was still unsure what career was the one for me. I had offers of places at both college and university to study librarianship but did not know if that was really what I wanted to do. That summer I had a holiday job with Dunbartonshire County Council as a library assistant and at the end of it was offered a permanent position. This seemed a good idea as it gave me time to think. As my year there came to its end I knew that the one thing I did not want to do was librarianship and I sent off an application to Aberdeen University to study for an MA in English literature. The goal I had in mind was to come out the other side as an English teacher.

Coming to faith

Years later I realised that God had been steering my life and career decisions even though I was totally unaware of it at the time. September 1975 saw me moving into a university residence in Aberdeen and sandwiched between two Christians who introduced me to a third. The four of us became friends and it was not long until I was going with them to a well known evangelical church in Aberdeen. It was there that I first heard expository preaching and I am in no doubt that it had a powerful effect on my life.

The biggest influence on me at that time was the Hall Bible Study Group which met once a week. I discovered what real Christianity was all about when I heard the testimonies of other young people my age who were believers. I think that the study group leader must have thought that I had become a Christian, and perhaps I thought so too, for he asked me to lead a Bible study during my first winter in Aberdeen. I went home to Bearsden for the week-end before the study was due and there spent Saturday afternoon preparing for it. The passage for study was Psalm 88 and one part of it in particular really stood out for me - the verses in which the psalmist begs God not to let him go down to the pit.

That night there was a particularly good film on television and because I wanted to see it I planned an early bath before settling down to watch it. It was there in the bath that I had a sudden and unexpected awareness of the presence of Christ outside of my life. I realised that that was where he was, for I had not yet personally invited him into my life. My knowledge of Christ was all in my head, I did not know him in my heart. I prayed a very simple prayer asking forgiveness and inviting him into my life, and on 29th February 1976 I became a Christian in the bath. Perhaps that is why I am a Baptist! But that is another story altogether.

I wish I could tell you that my life after becoming a Christian was one of constant growth in the Lord, but I cannot. During the long summer vacation back in Bearsden I was without fellowship as I did not settle in a church there. As a result it was with a distinctly cooler love for the Lord that I returned to Aberdeen. The coolness became a chill as I succumbed to bitterness because of some friends who I believed had let me down. I drifted far away from the Lord. My life fell to bits. And I felt so lonely that at one point I even contemplated suicide. Many students, especially those living away from home, go through similar experiences.

As I walked through Bearsden the following Easter I asked God to show me the way back to himself. Just then I passed a sign that I had not seen before saying 'Baptist Church' and I decided to ask some people who went to a Baptist Church in Aberdeen if I could go with them when I got back. All this time I had never stopped going to church, but there was no pleasure in it for my bitterness was a barrier blocking God out of my life.

The first time I attended Gilcomston Park Baptist Church, now Gerrard Street, Aberdeen, a baptismal service was being held. While watching the baptisms I realised that I had not really put my old life to death.

Having died to self when I became a Christian I had tried to go back to my old ways of life, my old patterns of behaviour. I knew then that I had to hand over my whole life to Christ, that I had to bury it and let him raise me to a new life altogether. I knew then that I needed to be baptised as a believer, and so I was in June 1977.

My spiritual life began to flourish and before long I found myself a youth leader with sometimes over 100 students and young people coming to meetings. Half of them even turned up for prayer meetings on Saturdays! My aim after graduating MA had been to leave Aberdeen and teach English; instead I remained in the city and studied for a Bachelor of Divinity degree while serving as Student Assistant Pastor for two years in my church. The congregation supported what was taken to be a clear call to the Baptist ministry. During my BD degree I had the privilege of living in digs with a Christian deaf couple and as a result of our friendship I learned sign language and developed a small ministry to the deaf.

Life as a pastor

In May 1982 I was ordained at Gilcomston Park and the following month began my first ministry at Ladywell Baptist Church, Livingston. By then I had faced the tragedy of losing my twin brother and his wife of only four months in a car accident. More positively I had married Kathleen and in 1983 our first child, Michael, was born. Michael's little sister, Amy, followed two years later.

I had five and a half years at Ladywell. The church

grew and the ministry was blessed. At that point the emphasis of my ministry was expository preaching, evangelism and administration. There were some very sticky moments, and some very painful pastoral problems, but it was a supportive church and a good start for my ministry.

In 1986 I asked the Lord for three more years in Ladywell. What I got instead was meningitis. The Sunday before taking unwell I had preached on Jonah. During the sermon I said that if we were going the wrong way with the Lord then he would send some great storm into our lives to bring us to our senses. Four days later I was in an ambulance on my way to hospital. The congregation loved it! One deacon reminded me what I had said but wisely added, 'You know, Ian, sometimes these things come to you when you are doing nothing wrong.' His remark and that time of serious illness gave me an insight into the experience of people who go through troubles which are not a direct result of wrongdoing on their part. That has definitely influenced my pastoral ministry.

Meningitis, however, seemed to bring the chapter at Livingston to a close. It did not surprise me, therefore, when in the summer of 1987 I was invited to begin a ministry in Peterhead and felt constrained to go. Peterhead was very different from Ladywell. It was traditional, Ladywell was modern. It had 300 members, Ladywell had 200. I count the first year of my ministry in Peterhead as one of the most exciting and privileged times of my life. Following a powerful Easter baptismal service we went on to baptise 75 people in three months. The church exploded in growth to the point that we could no longer easily fit our building. They were exciting days indeed.

It was then, when things seemed to be going well in the church, that things began to go wrong for me. There was undoubtedly a combination of factors. The congregation had grown substantially yet still had only one pastor and a decision was taken not to call other staff. Over the years of my ministry people opened more and more to me and I found myself trying to do the pastoral work of a large congregation and preach three times a week by myself. It was all downhill. I became exhausted and had two severe doses of 'flu'. And my father died suddenly. Perhaps it was not surprising that by May 1990 I felt I had no energy left.

Health problems appear

I returned from a two week preaching trip to New York with a tummy bug that would not clear. During that trip I had confessed to a friend that I was feeling stale in the ministry and had lost something of my sense of call. It seemed to me that I had been ministering for about six months with my foot on the brake. I had been burning out. As a result of this insight I gave my life to the Lord afresh and told him that he could do anything he liked with it. That prayer turned out to be one of the most dangerous I have ever prayed!

By the end of the summer I had recovered from the bug, but during the autumn months I felt worse than I had ever done in my life. The symptoms of my problem were bizarre and distressing. My temperature changed suddenly and unpredictably. Pins and needles plagued my arms and legs. My skin underwent terrible colour changes and wild and frightening dreams were in vivid technicolor. I felt such a dreadful fatigue that it seemed that my muscles would no longer support me.

There were times while I was working at the word processor when I could not even co-ordinate my hands and fingers. Words and thought just 'locked' in my head. Forgetfulness became a real problem but worst of all I sank into such a dreadful depression that I sometimes sat under my desk clutching my head and howled like a dog in pain and distress. Amazingly I managed to keep most of this awful experience hidden from my wife and family and the church leaders.

I found it almost impossible to discuss with others what was happening to me and I probably made it worse by hiding how I was really feeling. During this nine months of erratic health I felt that my GP was unsympathetic, that my wife did not understand, and that some of the church leaders were fed up with what was going on. Indeed one told me at a deacons' meeting that I was too young to be so ill for so long and was it not about time that I stopped delaying the inevitable. It was not so much the hurtful words, but the painful silence of the others that made it impossible for me to carry on.

In some ways I felt betrayed by people who ought to have supported me in a time of illness. Some church deacons and members came 'in love' and suggested that I either get better or get out. Others thought the problem was that the church was too big for me but they were unable to see that it was too big for any one person. I found myself agreeing with a doctor who in his book on Post Viral Fatigue wrote:

> Apart from its social status, employment has great emotional effect. With work, individuals feel that they are contributing to the community. They feel useful. They are playing their part. It is a team game and they are good to have on your team.
>
> Suddenly with PVFS, their role has been changed. Instead of a valuable member of the team, there is a handicapped one. Others have to do more work. The patient feels guilty. Not only is self esteem lost, but there is also the realisation that they are helped, tolerated, even patronised. Illness is compounded by guilt and self criticism. Many feel that they are given a gun, and asked to do the honourable thing - shoot themselves.[1]

That was exactly how I felt. I was a type A achiever, working long hours and aiming for perfection in everything I did. The carefully thought out sermons I presented to the congregation three times every week were to me a source of pride. But the church had grown, and pastoral needs were becoming more and more demanding on me, physically, spiritually and emotionally. The slightest hint of dissatisfaction put a tremendous amount

---

1. *Better Recovery From Viral Illness* by Darrel Ho Yen. Published by Dodona Books.

of self-generated stress upon me. My inability to get over a viral illness was the straw which broke the already heavily bent camel's back. I was an accident waiting to happen.

I now believe that God used my type of personality, and surrounded me with the kind of people who put pressure on me, in order to achieve his will. No longer do I see these terrible months of illness and 'betrayal' as the result of sinful men trying to bring down my ministry, but rather believe that God very carefully crafted me and those around me so that by using us together he achieved what he wanted in our lives. Although it is sometimes painful, God's will is always done.

Because I believed that God had given me no choice I asked to be released from my duties. My ministry in Peterhead finished on 2nd December 1990. I resigned in the firm belief that whatever was wrong with me was the beginning of a process of change in my life, and that when I came through to the other side it would not be to return to the job I was doing. There was no point in asking for leave of absence, the ministry at Peterhead for me was over.

For a few months nothing happened. Although Kathleen and I had a real sense of God's control, and believed that with his leadership we had taken the right decision together, we faced 1991 wondering what our next move was going to be. At the end of January I was finally diagnosed as having Chronic Fatigue Syndrome, or ME, and was advised not to work for at least a year.

The very next day Kathleen was offered a permanent

job as a secondary school teacher in Sanquhar in the south of Scotland, the children got the last two remaining places in their classes in the local primary school, and we bought a house. When we moved we found ourselves living beside another Christian couple with children the same ages as Michael and Amy. God's provision was perfect. We did indeed know his voice saying 'This is the way; walk in it' (Isaiah 30:21).

Recovery and a new place of service
There followed eighteen months of slow but progressive recovery. The little Baptist fellowship in Sanquhar was very supportive. With the pastor's gentle encouragement I remained in the ministry and took an occasional service. And along with some others we started up a youth work. I learned a lot about myself, my limitations, and where God has and has not gifted me. Having had the experience of being a house husband I have a whole new appreciation of the traditional woman's role in life! Actually, role swapping was a good idea. Kathleen earned more as a teacher than I did as a minister, and I kept the house cleaner than she did! Christian Focus Publications helped keep my brain alive by giving me some proofreading and editing work.

As far as the ME was concerned the thing that proved most helpful was time, although I also responded to anti-depressant medication. The 'space' which my illness gave me, linked to all I learned as a result of it, brought me full circle and saw the beginning of the ministry that I am in now.

Nearly two years before, just when I was poised to resign from Peterhead, the church there invited Liam Goligher from Kirkintilloch Baptist Church to do three days' Bible teaching. Liam and I enjoyed getting to know each other and I remember remarking to Kathleen as he drove off that I felt in some way our futures were linked. That thought went completely out of my mind as illness took over and we faced resignation, then the move to Sanquhar.

As my health improved the Lord began to put a fresh call into my life and two messages in particular spoke to me. The first was early in my stay in Sanquhar when the pastor preached on, 'Whenever you enter a house, stay there until you leave that town. And if any place will not welcome you or listen to you, shake the dust off your feet when you leave, as a testimony against them' (Mark 6:10-11). I realised that I had a lot of emotional 'dust' in my life which needed dealing with, and the Lord used a large part of my time in Sanquhar for that purpose. Later, towards the end of our stay there, a guest preacher spoke about Peter's restoration to ministry from John 21. I felt as though the Holy Spirit breathed in my sails and pushed me out into a new ministry.

The experience of having ME was a learning one and among the things I learned was this, that if I was going to minister it needed to be as part of a team, and that the emphasis of my work would be pastoral. In March 1992 I was approached by Liam Goligher and the church at Kirkintilloch with a view to joining their ministry team in a pastoral role. The call from the church was unanimous even though its members knew that I was not fully recovered from my time of illness. Not only was the Lord prompting me back into the ministry, but it seemed that he had also put a desire to encourage me back into the hearts of the people of Kirkintilloch. As a result I am now back in the full time work as part of the team at Kirkintilloch and am exercising a pastoral ministry which seems to be growing and deepening as time goes on. I can see that my present makes sense of, and makes use of the hard experiences I have been through.

I still have to be careful although I am now sufficiently recovered from ME to get better from illnesses reasonably well. And when I do have difficult days, they serve as reminders of how God has used the whole experience. Today finds me a very different person from the one I was four years ago. I believe that I am deeper, stronger and more mature and as a result more realistic in my expectations, both of myself and others. The emphasis of my ministry has changed. Then I would not have fitted into the team and the work in Kirkintilloch, now I do. God has used these years positively for the good. Having watched my old ministry die, it was as though it lay buried for two whole years before the tiny shoots of a new ministry began to appear. Although it was a waiting time for me, God was busy. I believe he has raised me up into a new ministry. He has helped me.

'Do you not know? Have you not heard? The LORD is the everlasting God, the Creator of the ends of the earth. He will not grow tired or weary, and his understanding no-one can fathom. He gives strength to the weary and increases the power of the weak. Even youths grow tired and weary, and young men stumble and fall; but those who hope in the LORD will renew their strength. They will soar on wings like eagles; they will run and not grow weary, they will walk and not be faint (Isaiah 40:28-31).

7

PRISCILLA MORGAN

How I wish my elders had realised the importance - indeed the necessity - of being human.

I made a decision for Christ as a little girl aged just seven. From then on my feet were never allowed to stray from the path on which I had so trustingly set them. It was assumed that I had no interest in, and no desire for, 'worldly' things. And it would have taken a braver child than I to stand against the current.

I grew up in a small, fervent, separatist community, with almost no other young people to dilute the attentions of our elders who were anxious to see that we grew up to be a credit to the deep teaching that we were privileged to receive. The things that other young Christians did, while perhaps legitimate for them, were not appropriate for us, for we were 'going on with the Lord'. To paraphrase the hymn - We had Christ, what more could we want?

There was very little difference between the daily lives of those who had reached a peaceful and sanctified old age and those of us who were living through artificially placid teenage years. Even contact with other young people at work or college was nullified, and the dangers of friendships with those who were not Christians was impressed upon us. Our own social cowardice also inhibited us - what, for example, if we were embarrassed by an invitation to the cinema? Even neutral events like sports were suspect. There was absolutely no common ground between us and other young people. And while we were all primed to the muzzle with sound teaching, somehow we were not very strong on sharing our faith with others.

The battle rages

As I grew older I realised that my earlier commitment had made no difference to my life at all, and I had the sense to know that it should have done. But I never dared admit this to anyone. I not only did not have the courage of my convictions - I did not have the convictions either. I was not an atheist, nor even an agnostic. I was very much a believer. I knew that what my elders lived was right and true. How could I say I just did not want it! Quite apart from the hurt it would cause, how could I face the pressure it would bring into my life? And being the preacher's daughter made it all very much worse.

So for most of my teens I lived the most rigidly conformist life. Although I was very unhappy about it, I could see no way out, unless I were to get genuinely saved, in which case my heart would be in it. I tried very hard, setting myself a tough programme of religious exercises, but God showed not the slightest interest in this kind of arm-twisting and eventually I gave up.

The victory won

Then, when aged nineteen, God became real and the vital force in my life. The pressure he put on me was almost physical. For weeks I fought a desperate battle with what I felt to be a threat to my precious identity - until one day the struggle was suddenly over. I am still not sure, in human terms, how it happened, but I knew I had come out into daylight. The relief was immense. I experienced the sheer happiness of contact with God, with a Person who knew me and cared about me, who really wanted me, nasty little hypocrite that I was. For some months I felt I was breathing real air for the first time in my life.

But I was still surrounded by my concerned and watchful elders. They were happy when I showed signs of growing up as a Christian, when I was baptised, when I prayed in public. They were my family in Christ, and I loved them. I knew how much I owed to their prayers. But somehow I kept stubbing my toes. I was hurt when I tried to discuss some enthralling book or idea I had come across, and was met with a worried frown and a suggestion that I would be better employed reading only my Bible. Almost everything was held to be a hindrance - even relationships with other Christians. But I truly wished to be a devoted follower of Jesus, to have nothing to do with things that were wrong. I remember being impressed by a sermon which stressed that Christ should be enough for us, even if we lived on a desert island. It was years before it occurred to me that Christ had not, in fact, put me on a desert island!

New beginnings

Some years later my holiday plans fell through, and my father offered to take me with him to a church conference. I have to admit that I went dragging my feet, thinking 'better than nothing'. The conference was a turning-point for me. I was challenged to a deeper commitment. And in the middle of it I met this fascinating man! I felt quite sure that this was a ploy of the devil to sidetrack me from important spiritual business and remember going up to my room one day and pleading with God to take that man out of my head. To my utter astonishment, a voice spoke very clearly into my mind, saying, 'Who says I want him out of it?' I could do nothing but sit back and gasp! I took this as no absolute guarantee of a happy ending - I just felt I could relax and not have to fight it.

But there was a happy ending. Two years later we married, and went to live a long way away. My husband, whose background was similar to my own, had spent a lot of time away from home and had a much wider range of experience. We started to build a life together outside of our accustomed framework because, although we were still heavily involved in Christian work, we were no longer in the centre of a separatist group. We felt a need, and an obligation because of my husband's profession, to mix socially with ordinary folk.

What a lot we had to learn! We found that a good deal of what we had absorbed about the world, about society, about ourselves as human beings, was quite inadequate and sometimes simply not true. And we have spent years relearning and rethinking. I lived through a fierce reaction against my early intense 'spirituality'. God never lost his grip of me, however angry I was with him or however remote I felt from him. I wholeheartedly accepted Christ but had real problems with what I saw as Christianity. And I was confused. I saw some devoted, single-minded Christians happily oblivious of sins which would be spotted at once by people not committed to the overlooking of one another's faults. And I was baffled to find among those I would have called 'heathens' qualities of kindness, open-heartedness, healthy-mindedness and unpretentious goodness that were like cold water in a drought.

Wilderness years

During a year of overwhelming personal trouble I had to withdraw from my rigid Christian friends for the sake of my own survival. I needed human kindness and warm-heartedness from whatever quarter they came, and at that time they came from those who would have balked at the thought of being Christians.

Then I read an article by a woman who had opted out of a very narrow religiosity, but felt that in doing so she had failed the Honours course, and would have to go through life as a second rate Christian. That was exactly how I had been feeling unconsciously. But to see it in cold print jolted me awake. I knew there must be more for me than this. I could not, in honesty, go back to the 'super-spirituality' I had found inadequate. But if God was who I thought he was, he could not leave me hopeless and defeated. There must be a place for me to go.

A small light flickered at the end of the tunnel when I read these words in T S Eliot's *Four Quartets*.

'I said to my soul, be still, and wait without hope
For hope would be hope for the wrong thing; wait without love
For love would be love of the wrong thing; there is yet faith
But the faith and the love and the hope are all in the waiting.'

The words spoke to me very directly. I stopped thrashing around. I stopped trying to figure where I could go. I put all my faith and love and hope into waiting, and then God showed me.

A Christian in the arts?

The question had come up, when I became a Christian, of my involvement in the arts. This was absolutely vetoed because of the worldly contacts I would make and because my artistic gifts were not seen to be a sufficiently overt witness to my faith. I hurt dreadfully. Because I believed that all my gifts came from God, I instinctively felt the decision to be wrong, but did not know how to say so. I saw it as my clear duty to obey my elders, so I did, thereby doing myself long-lasting harm. The springs of creativity gradually dried up, and my whole personality began to shrivel, though I did not then realise what was happening to me.

It took many unhappy years, a nervous breakdown, and a great deal of anguished thought before I realised that it was this hurt and rejection that was damaging me. Then God gave me back the creativity, and with it several striking confirmations that this was something he meant me to pursue.

By then my husband and I had really started to do some thinking. He had also grown up believing that one could not be an artist and a Christian, that one would have divided loyalties. But, as he watched my struggles, he said, 'If my idea of God can't cope with this, there is something wrong with my idea of God.' We began to see that I ought to be involved in my art. And then God did two remarkable things that confirmed this decision.

When I was 16, an uncle had drawn public attention to some work of mine, and as a result I had a little packet of newspaper clippings and letters that people had written me, which my mother kept in her desk. When I got married and left home I asked for it, but she said she rather thought she'd like to keep it herself. In those days, and in our circle, no daughter would have been so undutiful as to say 'But it's mine!' So I went away without it. Then, all those years later, something moved her to send it to me, and it arrived right in the middle of this crisis. The timing was staggering!

About this time we had a visit from the late Francis Schaeffer, who came in on all our discussing and said, 'But of course you should be involved.' What's more, he added, I did not have to strain to make my work consciously Christian. Anything, from making shoes to painting a picture, is to the glory of God if it's done truly and honestly and to the best of our ability.

We must, of course, accept God's ruling on what we are to do with our gifts and abilities. Sometimes he takes away something, but only to give us something else that he has chosen. He does not leave us deprived. But if we ourselves make such decisions, amputate bits of ourselves, either because of pressure from other Christians, or a wrong or inadequate view of the part we are meant to play in society, we will be left deprived. And deprived and frustrated people are strained, unhappy, not comfortable to be with - as I am sure I was myself during my wilderness years.

I had sometimes wondered, in my early days, what we had been put on earth for - what we were doing that could not be better done in heaven? Looking back, it seems to me that we had suffered from what I now call the 'left luggage syndrome' - the belief that our business was to stay put until either we died or Christ came to collect us, and meantime to form no links with the world around us. In straining every nerve to be 'spiritual' we were trying to lift our feet off the ground.

Christ's humanity - and ours

I started to read the life of Christ - from scratch and with no presuppositions. It was the most therapeutic thing I could ever have done. And how very different I found his earthly life to be from my preconceived notions of it. Jesus was a fully human being. He met people where they were. He went to parties when invited. And it did not worry him if people accused him of enjoying himself.

I had met, from time to time, and never forgotten some genuinely mature Christians whose obvious closeness to Christ had enhanced their humanity, had made them more individual and attractive people. This, I realised when I thought about it, is surely God's will for us - not that we should be less human, but more. I discovered that it is through Christ that we can break free from sin, from pressures to conform to the world, even the world as defined by some Christians, and be free to become the individual people God created us to be.

Derek Kidner wrote a book called *The Christian and the Arts* in which he says:

'For his neighbour's sake if for no other reason, the Christian should beware of becoming a person of so few earthly interests that he cannot even sustain a conversation, let alone a friendship, with anybody outside his religious circle. To have a genuine and discriminating pleasure in some human pursuit is to be halfway towards deserving human confidence; and without confidence people cannot be led towards the knowledge of Christ; they can only be prodded.'

I came to see that Christ took on humanity so that he could be the bridge between us and God. And it is through our humanity, redeemed by God, constantly directed by the Holy Spirit, that we are to show God to other people in terms they can understand.

So that is how I have been living my life ever since - as an ordinary human being - as a wife, a mother, now a grandmother, and as a friend. Also as an artist, where I have had a satisfying amount of acceptance - though there will always be people who will not give space to work that is motivated by a world view entirely different from the norm. My non-Christian fellow-artists can relax with me, for they know that I am not using my art to 'get at' them - I am not manufacturing propaganda. They know I share their aim to do the very best I can in my field, and this common commitment is a very strong link, strong enough most of the time to enable them to put up with my peculiar views in other areas, and sometimes even to listen.

It is amazing to me to look back and see what a revolution I have lived through. I had believed that, because God was all-important, nothing else should be allowed to matter. Now I see that it's because of God that everything matters. I see that God cares deeply for this creation and its affairs, and that he put us here to be useful and active parts of it. It is because of God that this world has come alive for me.

8

DAVID SPRIGGS

January 1st 1988 dawned slowly, as it usually does in the Scottish Highlands, having a little of the air of the 'day after the night before'. We had stayed up on Hogmanay with friends to pray in the New Year, and gone to bed soon after midnight. This crisp, clear, Friday morning my wife Joy and I were awake, but Simon (12), Stephen (10), Richard (8) and Emma (6) slept soundly, their dreams taking them into the unknown adventures of 1988.

'I wonder what this year has in store for us,' I mused.

'I wonder what God has in store for us this year,' Joy corrected.

As the wintry sun crept lazily above the hill behind our north-facing home overlooking the Moray Firth we lay in bed and reminisced. It seemed appropriate on the first day of the year to remember how good God had been to us over 16 years of marriage.

We both gave our lives to him in the mid sixties in Bristol, which was Joy's home town and where I studied dentistry. Joy's conversion took place at a youth camp and mine during a university mission several years before we met at 'Pip and Jay' (St Philip's and St Jacob's), a lively Anglican Pentecostal church in the centre of the city. We were to have ten very happy years

97

there learning about God and serving him. Then, in 1979, God very clearly led us to live and work in Inverness in the north of Scotland.

Looking back that New Year's Day morning we could see how true it was for us that 'in all things God works for the good of those who love him' (Romans 8:28). Although our marriage had been precious and blessed we had also known hard times: the cot death of our first-born son; a seemingly trivial accident that had left me with a small but significant disability; and other obstacles to overcome. We were left in no doubt that life had its ups and downs, but God had been with us in them all.

As we lay there talking, little did Joy and I know that 1988-9 was going to prove a milestone in our walk through life with Jesus and a time when God would sustain us with a special passage of Scripture, as he had done so often in the past, and prove to us again how good he is to his own.

The downward spiral

Big changes in my work as a clinical community dental officer for a large rural area resulted in longer working hours and a greater work load. The financial burden of a growing family meant that Joy had to take a small job. These, combined with the growing pains of a new church fellowship, seemed to conspire to create the 'not enough hours in the day' syndrome.

In March 1988 I took a heavy cold and suffered extreme tiredness. My doctor, a Christian, prescribed medication and told me to rest. She said she had prayed that I would do as she suggested then added, 'If you're not going to take my advice you had better tell me now so that I can go on praying!' I obeyed - reluctantly, improved a little, then returned to the stress cycle only to become ill again and be diagnosed as having ME a short time later. Such was my mind-set that instead of resting and letting the illness take its course I chose to fight it, the very thing I should not have done.

By October I was quite weak but still working every hour I could. A chest X-ray was taken, I had them three monthly, and was clear. At the end of November I visited my doctor yet again. 'Right David,' she said when I went in, 'let's pray.' We prayed. 'I did that,' she explained, 'because you look terrible.' 'I don't feel very well,' I had to admit.

She prescribed an antibiotic for my chest infection and I left. I was only halfway down the corridor when she called me back to tell me that although I was not due another X-ray, she felt the Lord was prompting her to have one done. It showed a fist sized tumour on my chest wall. Tests revealed cancer cells in my blood thus indicating the presence of some small secondaries.

As a dentist who has over the years specialised in treating children, especially nervous children, I think I know what fear looks like in someone's eyes, and I trust that I have, in my professional capacity, been able to reduce that fear to a minimum. There is probably no word which produces as much fear in the human heart as the word *cancer*, with all that it conjures up in our minds. When, at the beginning of December 1988, I was diagnosed as having terminal cancer I reacted with fear, that same fear I had seen in the eyes of a few of my young patients.

A hope and a future

My fear at that time was real, but God did not allow it to continue for very long. His peace is the most practical gift that he can give us in times of distress. In what could have been the most frightening and confusing time of my life, his peace enabled me to be realistic - something some of my non-Christian relatives and friends found very hard. Initially I expected that my faith and trust in God would take a bashing, I had seen that happen before over much smaller matters, but the reverse proved true. In this time of real adversity God seemed to strengthen my faith to face whatever was coming to meet me.

Somehow it seemed easier to trust in God with the distractions of life stripped away by cancer. And I found myself accepting that if it took me into eternity I should be as content as if I were to recover. At the same time God seemed to give me an immense, and for me uncharacteristic, strength to fight. He also gave Joy and me a promise from his Word over and over again. It was quite unmistakably for us and we clung to it.

It came first on the morning of my initial exploratory surgery in a letter from a friend in Nepal and it was repeated in letters and calls from all over the U K and beyond. 'I know the plans I have for you,' declares the LORD, 'plans to prosper you and not to harm you, plans to give you hope and a future. Then you will call upon me and come and pray to me and I will listen to you. You will seek me and find me when you seek me with all your heart. I will be found by you,' declares the LORD, 'and will bring you back from captivity' (Jeremiah 29:11-14). Every set of tests, every exploratory operation, every session of treatment and every hospital visit was preceded by the gift of these same verses from someone or somewhere. God clearly and lovingly assured us that he was in control and that we need not fear - whatever the future held.

Dates from my diary

Looking back I am amazed at how much there was to do and more than that, how much there was to pray about. God had drawn so close that Joy and I decided to share with him every detail of my condition and treatment and how I felt about it. God knew it all already, but it helped us to ask his blessing and commit each detail to his care. With that in view I requested that my doctors share their thoughts about the progress of the treatment and these were recorded in a prayer diary. As I had never kept a diary before (and, incidentally, have not done since), I was unsure even how to begin. In the end I resolved to address the diary to God.

Mid December - 'Lord, they think it is a thymoma again today. Last Wednesday it was a lymphoma and the week before it was a thymoma. They don't seem very decided about what they are going to do or what it is. Please can you make them understand.' Just a few days later a definite diagnosis was given. I was suffering from a lymphoma.

We prayed about the tumour, that it would simply stop growing. On December 24th, the consultant in Aberdeen having conducted a thorough examination and biopsy reported on his findings. 'It's quite remarkable. It has stopped growing, you know.' I wanted to tell him that I did indeed know! He went on, 'And what's more it has changed consistency quite considerably. It's quite different from what it was. And the blood test - we've found some peculiar cells, but we can't find anything like the number of cancer cells that were floating around before.'

I felt very weak and ill when I confided in my diary early in January 1989. 'Lord, they are going to try radiotherapy, but I can tell from their faces they aren't really very sure. Lord, you know what's the right thing. Could you please show them what sort of treatment I should have?'

It was decided that radiotherapy would be appropriate but, when I turned up for my first session, I was admitted for chemotherapy. I believe God guided that change of plan. I was keen for the treatment to start; when it did however, an old problem returned. As soon as the apparatus was prepared for the drip something welled up inside me, something I've always suffered from desperately - needle phobia. Many years ago I thought that if I became a dentist I would be cured of it, but was not. I had just about coped with the blood tests, even the needle biopsies, but now I was in deep trouble.

Of all the things I met during these eight months of treatment none inspired more fervent prayer than my fear of needles.

'Lord,' my diary records one day in March, 'I'm giving up. I can't face any more.' Despair was never far below the surface. At the time treatment was going well and the consultant was pleased with my progress. I felt more confident and the picture was altogether brighter. What provoked that entry? A locum doctor had been a little rough with me. One small lapse of kindness tipped the balance and I wanted no more than to be left to die. I knew of other patients who had chosen to abandon their treatment and they did die. God graciously provided a very patient nurse who talked me into continuing.

Discouragements and encouragements

My illness and treatment took its toll of the family. Like their parents, our children had committed their lives to Christ, but my heart was full of concern for them. They were under such a lot of stress because of me. God answered our prayers for them by providing wonderfully supportive Christian friends. One newly married couple was even brave enough to take Simon, Stephen, Richard and Emma on holiday with them for a week.

Cancer, I discovered, stripped me of life's little extras. Even as Christians we collect many things around us which so easily take up more time than they should. Cancer pushed them into the background leaving the basics, the two most important matters in my life - my relationship with God and my relationship with other people. I found that the main desires in my heart were to see people I had prayed for over the years come to faith in Christ; to see their problems sorted out; and to put right relationships that I knew were not as they should be. The result was much prayer and a vast amount of letter writing. Inverness Post Office must have recorded an increase both in its turnover and its profits.

Chemotherapy had some side effects. I had been told my hair would fall out. It did, apart from the areas of my arms where the needles were inserted which needed shaving before each treatment! My beard went quickly but not my moustache. One day, when I was out of hospital between treatments, I met a patient of mine in town. As we chatted I had a terrible itching sensation in my upper lip. I scratched it to relieve the itching and continued the conversation. A little while later, as I waited for the bus, I caught my reflection in the plate glass of the Post Office window. Where a whole moustache had been only half of one remained. I tugged quite hard at what was left but it stayed put, and I still had to get the bus home!

'It was good to see Jonathan again today, Lord,' I wrote in my diary. Visitors were vital and some were exceptional. Jonathan came every second Thursday at exactly 10.30 am. We chatted, had coffee then prayed together for an hour. Elaine, a Christian neighbour, popped in for ten minutes every single day. I believe that their regularity and reliability were inspired by God. I was fortunate to have a lot of visitors but found that, although I have always been a gregarious sort of person, coping with cancer made me rather shy and reticent. And inwardly I became less trusting and, I think, less tolerant. The visitors I found most helpful were those who treated me normally, mentioning cancer quite naturally in the conversation. They helped me keep reality and faith in perspective.

Encouragements also came from unexpected quarters. The area I cover as a community dental officer extends over eleven small communities dotted around two valleys and eight mountains. The people in these communities rallied round wonderfully. Meals were left on our doorstep and other gifts given. Letters came from children in the schools I serve and from their parents too. The pupils in one primary school prayed for me throughout my treatment. I went to visit them while I was still off work. 'Look, boys and girls,' said the infant teacher when I went into her room, 'look who's here.' They didn't recognise me. Then the light dawned on one little boy's face. 'Miss,' he called out, 'it's Mr Spriggs with no hair on!' Many of the doors that opened in these communities during the course of my illness have remained open, giving me a new freedom to witness to my faith and to God's goodness.

As the months went on I became weaker, but Joy wisely recognised that, however little strength and energy I had, I needed to have tasks to do. I could manage the vacuuming, a little cooking and the shopping from time to time. Some friends shared her insight and gave me people and situations to pray for. Being given specific and necessary things to do made me feel both normal and useful - two things cancer steels from you if you let it.

My doctors were pleased with what was happening to the tumour, it was decreasing quite rapidly and eventually disappeared. Throughout that period I was prayed for constantly and the elders of my church laid hands on me and anointed me with oil several times. There was no dramatic miracle of healing, but I was nevertheless getting better against all odds. It was beginning to seem possible that I might survive.

'I believe your cancer is in remission,' said the consultant in June 1989. 'But take great care, it could return any time given the right circumstances. You must change your lifestyle and cut out all the stress you can.' It was good to know that the lump in my chest had gone, but the idea of being in remission began to disturb me. Had God healed me or was this temporary? It was only remission. Being cured would have been better. Certainly it would have felt much safer, remission sounded a little dangerous. It might come back at any time and I didn't think I could face the treatment again.

The doctors offered a little hope in that they said they would give me tests every few months for ten years and, if they found no sign of the cancer returning, would then pronounce me cured. God reminded Joy and me again of his promise to give us a hope and a future. I may be only in remission, but remission is a good place to be, the best in fact, for it is where God wants me. Here I can never rely on man's wisdom or expertise, only God's power to heal.

I had already demonstrated that I could be less than sensible about my health if left to my own devices. In remission I had no option but to be careful and respect the new lease of life God had given me. Perhaps more importantly, in remission my testimony to God's healing grace is always fresh and up to date. He it is who keeps me there.

What after cancer?

I was back at work three weeks after my course of chemotherapy was completed and I am still working five years on. That I should be here so long after a diagnosis of aggressive terminal cancer is too wonderful for me to put into words. But even greater is the privilege of God's closeness to my family and myself during those difficult days. Looking back to his goodness at that time enables us to look forward echoing the sentiments of David, the psalmist, 'Even though I walk through the valley of the shadow of death, I will fear no evil for you are with me; your rod and your staff they comfort me' (Psalm 23:4).

I don't know why God brought me through this experience, but I do know that one result of it is that I have to encourage others who are walking along the road I have walked. For most people cancer produces a sharp negative picture, but I believe that with the right counsel, the right sensible medical approach, and the right sensitive spiritual help, God can make the picture positive. That has been my experience. Cancer became a means through which God could bless both me and my family. One direct outcome of my time of illness has been that Joy was offered a job in the Highland Hospice. She is able to bring a sensitivity and understanding to her work there which was born of what we have gone through together. In the world's eyes cancer produces victims, in God's eyes it creates opportunities - whatever the outcome.

9

RITA ARMSTRONG

Early childhood memories are so happy! My home in Southampton spelt shelter and security, whilst friendly rivalry with Bernard, my older brother, only served to add spice to life. Father worked in Pirelli's, Mother was busily involved in church work and Gran lived with us. I remember happy school days, walks on Southampton Common and sand-between-the-toes holidays.

But all that ended abruptly with the outbreak of World War Two on 3rd September 1939.

Although I was only eight years old I sensed something of the enormity of the situation and crept into the lounge to kneel beside the settee and pray. I can still feel the roughness of uncut moquette, the edge of the carpet square on a grazed knee, but I cannot remember what I prayed. Would it have been a childish plea to take the naughty war away? I don't remember. But I do know that God was very real, very relevant.

On the move

Compulsory evacuation to Bournemouth ended the stability as families were loathe to have strange children billeted on them. Because schools could not cope with the sudden influx of pupils, local children had classes each morning while evacuees had theirs in the afternoons. But for Bernard and me this situation only lasted a few months as we joined our parents at Christmas in a rented house in South Harrow.

It was so cold there, that a trifle froze to slivers of ice in the pantry and a burst pipe caused consternation as well as a flood. Then we spent a few weeks with a pernickety aunt who drove my mother mad, but who taught me to embroider crinoline ladies, turn a heel on socks destined for sailors on the high seas, and sing 'improving' Victorian songs.

Before long we moved with Gran to Bromley near Biggin Hill Airfield. We only lived there for a year but it seemed longer as so much happened. Soon after settling in, all five of us went to visit aunts in Charlton. Bernard and I knew the long bus journey took us nearer London with its exciting memories of Trafalgar Square, Buckingham Palace and Madame Tussaud's, but no such treat awaited us that day. This was a duty call to spend the afternoon being polite to elderly relatives.

Lunch was a formal affair but as soon as possible we escaped into the garden to watch men in the park across the road as they freed a floppy, silver barrage balloon, to float high above our heads like an inverted puppet on its snapping strings. An air-raid warning had us scurrying indoors to find whatever shelter we could. Warnings were still a novelty and there was a sense of excitement as, like a bizarre game of hide and seek, aunts disappeared under the table, we hid behind the sturdy settee and Gran, who was only small, buried herself in the depths of the under-stairs cupboard.

Bernard and I played 'cats cradle' and 'I spy', but gave up because we couldn't spy the same things and, anyway, the noise of planes became deafening. He amused himself guessing the kind of aircraft overhead.

'Mum, I want the toilet,' I wailed.

'You'll have to wait.'

'But you said that ten minutes ago!'

'Can't be helped - you'll just have to wait.'

It was dark when we eventually emerged, stiff and solemn, to a strangely silent world. Towards London an eerie light lit the sky like a fierce sunset. As we trekked home I was appalled to see people whose houses and gardens overlooked the devastation charging folk for a better view from their windows or garden walls. We trudged on, saddened and subdued, wondering if our house would still be intact, while Gran struggled to keep up with us on her short bow-legs.

A child's eye view of war

The phoney war had ended and we all pondered what lay ahead. What I did not realise till many years later was that for me a private battle was about to begin.

Sirens became commonplace. Shelters, both indoors and out, grew almost cosy through constant use. Bombs whistled down. Windows, protected by crosses of tape, were blown out and repaired - only to be shattered again and replaced by boards. Sammy, my precious doll, was smashed. Ceilings came down and everything, including food, was covered with a fine film of dust.

In our youthful innocence, Bernard and I played a

game. As soon as the all clear sounded we hurried out to see the damage, watching stretchers being carried out, counting those with blankets over their heads. One evening we were first on the scene at a temporary fire station where the men had become our friends. We were horrified to see shiny black boots protruding from the rubble. Suddenly the game turned horribly sour.

People became disorientated. The threat of unexploded bombs was even worse than explosions. One land mine, caught by its parachute in a tree, caused chaos. The warden, a neighbour transformed by his battle dress and ARP hat, knocked us up in the early hours, shouting, 'Two minutes. Bus at top of road. One small case each. No pets.'

In dressing gowns and siren suits we piled into old buses to be taken to dusty church halls, where we sat on hard wooden seats, ate hard biscuits, drank strong tea and waited - wondering if there would be a home to return to in the morning. No-one slept, but nobody talked. Apart from the girning of a baby we shared our suffering in silence.

As most of the congregation of our local church moved away our family helped hold the fort. Small midweek house meetings were held as nobody wanted to go far afield. Our home hosted a Junior Christian Endeavour meeting and it was there that I learned to speak and pray aloud. In those days, even as a child, faith did not seem optional.

Cracks begin to show

But I had my own problems. During 1940 I started to bite my nails and, worse still, to wet the bed. It was embarrassing and, anyway, my mother had enough on her hands without extra washing. For a while we had Belgian refugees staying with us and she also had the worry of my father. He had chosen the option of coming home soon after surgery when the London Hospital in which he was a patient was evacuated. I was allowed to watch, fascinated, as our doctor dressed his deep wound every day - with Father's chair sometimes surrounded by debris.

By 1941 we all slept on make-shift beds and bunks in a downstairs room strengthened from floor to ceiling by huge oak beams. Only the cat slept in the next room curled up in my old wicker chair. One night a bomb that landed very close blew off all the doors and part of a wall as well. Mother was horrified when daylight came to find a door lying on top of Tigger's smashed chair. The cat was nowhere to be seen. He appeared later, dazed and dusty. He must have jumped - or been blown - out of the French window before the inner door fell.

The bed-wetting and nail-biting continued and I became accident-prone. Bruises and stitches were commonplace. Soon friends hardly recognised me without a sling on my arm! School work deteriorated. Piano lessons were abandoned. Hobbies remained unfinished. Outbursts of tears were not uncommon and decision-making became a problem. 'Mu-um! What shall I we-ar?' was a constant cry.

Depression's dark cloud

When Doodlebugs appeared in 1944 with the added torture of that dread silence as the engines cut out minutes before the explosion, I went to pieces and was immediately evacuated to a village near Loughborough. After a couple of unpleasant experiences with digs I ended up happily billeted at a Baptist manse and spent six rewarding months there. Most of the time I was a lively, out-going teenager but every now and again life lost its zest and I became weepy, anxious and withdrawn. Soon after I returned home Mother took me, discreetly, to visit a Christian doctor in a neighbouring town, but the Dexedrine tablets (pep pills) he gave me made me feel funny so I threw them down the toilet.

Twice the Black Dog, as Churchill called depression, crippled me during my nursing training. The second time Matron gave me two weeks leave of absence, advising me to go to the coast to 'blow the cobwebs away.' I was a practising Christian, keen to serve my Lord, and it puzzled me that during these dark times I could neither communicate with my Lord nor enjoy fellowship with other Christians.

When I was twenty I fell in love with Ron, a Scots student at the local theological college, and although I was not thrilled at the prospect of becoming a minister's wife, I wanted to marry him and believed this was the way the Lord was leading us. Surely, I thought, being in love, getting married and having my own home would solve all my problems.

But that was not to be. After the excitement of our

wedding and the busy-ness of setting up house the old feeling of being in a dark tunnel returned with all its isolating pain. People were puzzled by my occasional absences and Ron kept up the pretence by explaining that I was 'Just a bit under the weather'. I was certainly under a dark and heavy cloud. It was then that I began to hear remarks like, 'Pull yourself together,' 'Your husband needs you,' 'Everybody gets down a bit sometimes.' Sinister hints about something between me and my Lord upset me. Latterly there were people simply itching to lay hands on me for my healing!

Nothing could disguise the condition when early in my first, planned pregnancy, I became very depressed and sick. But once the first three months were over I positively bloomed with health until the birth of our son and, thankfully, no post-natal problems arose. Then came the day my doctor arrived as I lay sick in bed at the start of my second pregnancy. Without a word to me he shook his head sadly and knelt to pray. I felt so wretchedly ashamed and guilty and shrivelled in the bed, convinced that all this was my fault, I was an abject failure. I vowed never to seek the advice of a Christian doctor again.

Most of the time we were happy as a little, growing family. I learned to hide my 'downs' and soldier on. Our second pastorate was in Scotland, not far from Ron's home and, apart from periods of the now well-guarded secret, life was good. In times of crisis I could generally cope and we survived childhood ailments, household emergencies, even the day when Ron's routine visit to hospital resulted in a never-to-be-forgotten phone call. 'We're keeping your husband in,' Sister said. 'Operating tomorrow. He'll be off work 6 months - so bring his diary in this evening because you'll have to cancel all his engagements. Visiting's 7 to 7.30. Goodbye.'

It was more like a year before Ron was back to full health. Then once again he became expert at making excuses when depression made it impossible for me to cope. As we moved to churches around the country various doctors prescribed different anti-depressants, but none of the tablets made any difference. The black mood always lifted of its own accord after a few months.

Further pregnancies led to intravenous feeding and bed rest in hospital. On one such occasion I was transferred briefly to a psychiatric ward. It was quite an experience. The old army hut behind the main hospital blocks was packed with truckle beds alternating with lockers. As I was transferred one evening by stretcher my fellow patients assumed I had attempted suicide.

During that short stay two important things happened. First my mother unlocked the closet door behind which was hidden my family history. Tearfully she told me that her father had been shell-shocked during the Boer war, was frequently sent away for 'rest cures' and - prolonged pause - took his own life when she was 14. His sister also committed suicide after the birth of her son. And I already knew of a depressive uncle.

I was devastated.

But the Lord is very gracious and while I was feeling such a total failure a second important thing happened which gave me some encouragement. The girl in the next bed had noticed the unopened Bible on my locker and, like pulling teeth, she 'extracted' my testimony from me. I told her how, when I was only seven, I had caused some consternation by going forward at an evangelistic rally to tell the evangelist that I had given my heart to Jesus. As the organisers had not expected children to respond they hurriedly looked out some suitable material. Nobody took this solemn, dark-haired little girl very seriously. I overheard someone say, 'How sweet.' But I knew that Jesus loved me and could begin to understand that he died for me at Calvary. I certainly loved him and wanted to give him my whole life.

Whether this story helped my friend I will never know, but telling it to her put new heart in me, reminding me that God was present even in that dread place and could make me strong when I was at my weakest.

But my built-in suspicion of psychiatry was deep rooted. I discharged myself, went home, and laughed at the thought that our loo would never be depressed - the number of tablets that were consigned to it!

It was after the birth of our fourth and last child, a sickly baby, that 'high' spells began to alternate with 'lows'. I was bewildered. At times I felt I had a hot line to God while at others he did not seem to be there at all. Guilt and shame piled high as I struggled to function in public only to crawl home too exhausted to care for my growing family. I felt a hypocrite for publicly addressing prayers to God when he didn't seem to be listening. At other times I talked too much, drove dangerously fast, flirted uncharacteristically and spent money like water.

One middle-of-the-road day I plucked up courage to seek the advice of my doctor but received no help at all. 'It's your personality, dear,' he said brightly. 'Nothing I can do.' As I crawled from the room he called cheerfully, 'Good luck!'

Was there no help? No understanding?

Fighting back

But God was at work behind the scenes. In 1974 a Christian doctor in the partnership, whom I had avoided, read my notes, contrived an interview and showed concern. For the first time ever the cork came out the bottle and I found the whole sad story spilling over. He simply listened and empathised. On a second visit he involved Ron. We discussed the whole matter frankly and were gently persuaded that expert help was needed. He arranged for a psychiatrist to make a home visit and that was the first step in a totally new phase of my life.

We faced that dread diagnosis, 'manic-depression' or bipolar depression, and learned something about it. We discovered that it often, though certainly not always, runs in families; that one can be born with a tendency to it but never actually become ill and that some people only have one spell of illness while others, like me, suffer recurring swings. And when I learned that the illness is often triggered by a prolonged period of stress, I thought back to the trauma and fear of my war-time childhood.

'Treatment's come a long way since your grand-father's day, my dear,' the dapper psychiatrist told me.

'No more rest cures, no more restraints. Most people respond well to a trace element called Lithium. Not a drug - a chemical, like magnesium, potassium, that sort of thing. Acts on the brain cells. Chemical balance - delicate, see?' He made mood swings sound so very normal. 'Like over-steering a car, but we can control all that.' Apparently regular blood tests would be needed to monitor the level of Lithium in my blood. 'Like diabetics on insulin,' I suggested and he nodded.

It seemed so simple - a couple of pills a day and not a hint of undermining my Christian faith! Why had I been so scared? It would take a while to feel the benefit, we were told, but it offered real hope. For the first time we were cautiously optimistic.

Around this time I was introduced to an Edinburgh doctor called Winifred Rushforth. One of the first women to train in medicine, she became interested in psychotherapy and still, although aged 95, consulted privately. Quite incredibly she was then writing a book and was working on a second when she died the following year. Winifred believed in each one of her patients and helped us to believe in ourselves. My bruised and battered personality was bathed in her loving acceptance. She was never shocked. She never told us what we ought to do. She did not tell us - she showed us that God loved us.

Meditation

By now my children had grown up and were leaving home. One afternoon, as I sat in a rare moment of peace meditating on God's greatness and power, I thought back to the blitz, then scanned through the centuries to Calvary, and back still further to the beginning of everything. And only God was there. Then I contemplated the future, the time when my life would come to an end, and forward to the day everything would finally be wound up. And God would still be there. I felt very insignificant against such a backcloth and my petty problems paled pathetically. Then I remembered the childlike faith with which I had given my young life to God, confident that Jesus loved me. And Jesus cannot change. He is the same yesterday, today and forever.

Suddenly a light shone. Realisation dawned and a great joy overwhelmed me. Something I must have been told many times became real and I started to dance around the room. It must have looked a ludicrous sight - a plump, middle-aged matron cavorting about all on her own! But what I was singing over and over was quite simply this, 'I matter to God! I matter to God!'

That was fifteen years ago and, after a period during which my mood swings gradually stabilised, I began to feel a different person. Of course I am far from perfect, and readjustments have been needed, not least within the family. But I feel accepted and whole. Although some people only require a short course of Lithium, often combined with other drugs, I seem to need continuous treatment and am content to accept that for the rest of my life, should it prove necessary.

There has been just one spell of illness which necessitated a five week stay in a psychiatric ward. I was angry, agitated, anxious and suspicious of my loved ones. For a while my confidence was shattered, but it was restored when I read that a sleeping tablet prescribed for me had been removed from the market for causing the symptoms from which I was suffering.

These years have not lacked trauma. Seven years ago our youngest son died suddenly of leukaemia. He was just 23 years old. At first, as I thought of that difficult pregnancy, the fight to keep him alive in infancy, the problems during his teens, I did ask God, 'Why?' But as I looked again at the cosmic plan of our almighty, loving God and reminded myself that even a pathetic manic-depressive mum matters to him, I could do nothing but worship and adore him.

I have come to rely more and more on times of relaxation and Christian meditation, lifting my thoughts to my sovereign God, reminding myself not only of his awe-ful majesty but of the fact that he loves and cares for me.

After seeking qualified approval I began to hold support groups for other Christians with emotional needs. Many believers who suffer from depression find that their problems are compounded by guilt and shame. But Jesus said, 'Come to me, all you who are weary and burdened, and I will give you rest' (Matthew 11:28).

'Can't think of anything worse than a roomful of depressives!' a friend commented. She should come and see. We almost always have a great deal of fun and the fellowship is tremendous.

But this world is not my home and, good as this life

may be, I can't wait to reach my everlasting home in heaven. Unlike my war-torn childhood homes it will offer unshakable security. 'Here we do not have an enduring city, but we are looking for the city that is to come' (Hebrews 13:14). And I rest on what Jesus said about it: 'In my Father's house are many rooms ... I am going there to prepare a place for you' (John 14:2-3).

10

DAVID AND RUTH KAY

'You know, Ruth,' my friend said, 'you'll just get this garden finished and the Lord will move you and David on.' I followed her up the narrow path in silence, pushing the thought to the back of my mind, and went in to make coffee. It had taken four years to rescue the garden from a history of neglect with all six of us involved in the family project. We dug out debris and carted away boxes of broken glass, numerous bed frames and what seemed to us a houseful of furniture, sadly thrown into the sloping garden and eventually buried.

I found myself repeating my friend's comment occasionally to visitors, most of whom asked, 'How's the garden going?' But it was Abigail, our youngest daughter, whose honest question really forced me to think the matter through. 'Will the Lord move us on, Mum?' she asked. It would be nearly two years before she had her answer but the 'shiftings' had begun.

Abigail asked her question four years after we left an Evangelical Mission with which we had worked for ten years, four of them full-time. We had not expected our service to be cut short but God quite clearly showed us that his plan for us lay in a different direction. To be turned around in the dark is never easy. It disorientates and makes us fearful of making a wrong move. I asked myself all sorts of questions and asked God some too. What is next, Lord? Where will we live? What about the children? Charlotte was then 15, Simon 13, Fraser 11 and Abigail 8, and they too were having their young faith tested.

A few years earlier, when I was worrying over another change of school, I asked the Lord for assurance, and was given it in my daily Bible reading: 'As for these four children, God gave them knowledge and skill in all learning and wisdom...' (Daniel 1:17 AV). At times like these it has helped me to remember what my choicest desires are for my children, not that they might fulfil any secret ambition I may have for them, but that God might graciously draw them to himself and prepare them for the future he has planned for them. This time of family uncertainty made us very aware of our dependence on God and encouraged our young folk to trust him too.

At the same time my mother's health began to deteriorate as she developed congestive heart disease. It became evident that she would increasingly need help, although she continued to live alone and uncomplainingly trusted her Saviour for each day's strength. As he saw her become more frail David wondered aloud, 'Perhaps the Lord will not move us away until he has taken Mum home to be with him.' That needed no comment, and I was to recall it a few years on.

Mother had been widowed quite suddenly eleven years previously. Dad went into hospital for routine, relatively minor, surgery. Suspecting something more serious, the surgeon ordered further tests, and a few hours later Dad underwent surgery for a serious heart condition without which, we were told, he would not last the week. He did not last the night. Towards the end of what was thought to have been successful surgery he suffered a heart attack. The surgeons had lost a battle, but for Dad the battle was over and won. All the trials of life were past and he was in heaven with his Lord. But for us who were left it was a loss, especially for my mother. She lost her life partner and a lot more too. Since my father, only 62, was still in full-time Christian work, the house, the car, the income and her role as a missionary wife went too.

Her assurance that 'the Lord will provide' was an example I remembered when our own time of uncertainty came along. In the midst of it, on a summer day in 1992, David and I found a quiet spot in the garden where we could pray about our future.

David tells of the 'waiting years'
Leaving the mission meant no home, no car and no income. So in August 1987 the six of us returned to Swindon, our 'home base' and to the church which had commissioned us. We looked for, and found, understanding. Ruth's mother occupied our little house so there was no room for us there. But God provided for our need when an American missionary couple returned to the USA, thus vacating a house which had been made available for missionaries on furlough and other Christian workers in need. As the house was well equipped our own furniture went into storage - until when, we

wondered. The mission car had to be returned early in September, but a friend at church lent us a car, tax-paid and insured until we could afford one.

I was in a dilemma. For five weeks I was registered unemployed and, although I was available to do any work, none came along. This was a burden we shared together. Did the ground ever feel shaky beneath our feet? Ruth will tell you that it did.

Over to Ruth

I wouldn't be honest if I said otherwise. We knew someone else needed the house within a few months. What if there was no job? Where would we live? It is not every family that numbers six! The Bible really spoke to me and I clung to verses like, 'Lord, you have been our dwelling-place throughout all generations' (Psalm 90:1). And over and again God reminded me that it is he who gives us security, not bricks and mortar. At one such time of doubt I discovered afresh the truth of Psalm 71:3: 'Be my rock of refuge, to which I can always go; give the commandment to save me, for you are my rock and my fortress.' I was reassured that I could always go to the God who copes when I could not.

David takes up the story

I knew God was calling me to full-time ministry and wondered whether he had a pastorate waiting for me. This seemed a possibility when a church in the north of England invited me to spend a month taking services and getting to know the congregation. In an independent church a prospective pastor is recommended to the members by the elders or deacons and the members then vote. At the end of that month the church members met to make their decision. As the time had gone well we were perplexed when, by a narrow margin, they did not call me. We wondered what the Lord had in mind. It was December 1987 and as I faced a new year still unemployed I was tremendously helped by two verses of Scripture: 'He (God) knows the way that I take; when he has tested me, I shall come forth as gold' (Job 23:10); and, 'He performeth the thing that is appointed for me, and many such things are with him' (Job 23:14 AV).

While the Bible reminded me that God was completely in control and that as head of the family I had to trust in his providence, it nowhere said that I should do nothing to help myself and my family. Five other people were depending on my leadership. Called to ministry I might be, but I had other callings too - those of husband and father. It was my place to provide for my wife, physically, emotionally and spiritually. Similarly, as a father, I knew I should provide as best I could for my children's need of stability, security, educational opportunity and spiritual welfare. I wondered what to do. Should I continue to seek a full-time ministry whilst remaining unemployed, or take a secular job which, by its very nature, would limit my availability for ministry?

Until 1983 I worked in the National Health Service as a nurse teacher. Was that a possibility? With that in mind I contacted a former colleague and office-mate, the Senior Nurse of the psychiatric clinic, and we spent two happy hours reminiscing. I explained my situation and wondered whether he had any junior trained nurse positions available. A letter which arrived two days later read, 'Following your interview today I am pleased to offer you a full-time position as a Staff Nurse.' Interview?

I was grateful to God, and to Bill, for the work. It was a humbling but helpful experience to be on the bottom rung of the ladder, taking orders from nurses who had been my students years before. And it allowed me to re-orientate in the light of the changes which had taken place in the NHS during my time away. After three months I was asked to fill in at an industrial therapeutic workshop as nurse manager, then again to fill in for a community psychiatric nurse who was away on a course. Then amazingly, in June 1988, I was invited by the Director of Nurse Education to come back to the School of Nursing as a Nurse Teacher, to the very job I had left five years before.

Ruth remembers
As we prayed in the garden I heard David telling the Lord that we were willing to stay put in Swindon and to remain in secular employment if that was his will. We were subdued by the seriousness of the prayers we had prayed.

Just a few days later David received a phone call asking him to speak at an evangelistic barbecue in Salisbury. It seemed a reassurance to him that the Lord was calling him to the work of the gospel. So it was that we went as a family to the barbecue, joining about sixty others there to hear the gospel message that David was able to give. A man from North Devon who was holidaying in the area with his family engaged David in conversation. He was genuinely amazed - David's name had been given to his church as a possible preacher some months before; yet he had come to the barbecue in Salisbury not realising that he was to listen to this very man! An invitation to preach at that North Devon evangelical church followed seven months later, in January 1993.

David visits Devon

It is a special joy to have time away with just one of your children. Leaving Ruth and the others behind, Abigail and I set out for Barnstaple and spent a very happy weekend there. The warmth of the welcome was touching, as was the congregation's love for God's Word. 'Do they have a pastor?' Ruth asked casually when we told her how much we had enjoyed our visit. She made no comment on my answer. 'No, and I don't think they're looking.' The beginning of March brought a real surprise, a phone call asking if I would consider returning to Barnstaple, to preach 'with a view' as they say!

I needed space to seek God's will. Having agreed to give an answer within a few days I spent a long four days. Doubts and fears raised their heads and questions cried out to be answered. Do I really want a move now? After all, 46 is perhaps a little late for a career change. What about my local church? My fellow elders - what will they think? My dear wife, Ruth, was an experienced 'mover' but this would be her 25th home.

I had to think of the children - all five of them now. Six months previously we had received approval from the Social Services Department to have Angelina, aged 11, to live with us long-term. She very quickly became part of the family. But that meant I had another life to consider. How would this affect Angelina? Would the authorities allow her to move at all? What about her natural family? They needed to be considered too.

About this time it became evident that Angelina would feel more at home with us if she no longer had the supervision and restrictions that come along with the care of a child who is fostered. We received tremendous support from Lyn, Angelina's social worker, who almost became a friend of the family! But even Lyn, fond of Angelina as she was, could see that she needed to live as normal a life as possible.

We were encouraged to apply for a Resident's Order which releases a foster-child from the supervision of the Social Services, including regular visits to the foster home, by placing parental responsibility with the foster parents. In Angelina's case this responsibility is shared with her father, although in practice it falls to us as she only sees him four or five times a year. He was happy to see her settled despite moving away. The exciting prospect of moving with a family, and not in or out of one, was viewed as positive, and we were assured that should we need support from Social Services in Devon it would be available. This has proved to be a real step forward for Angelina, although not without its problems.

And there was Ruth's mother. What I had said to Ruth

about Mum came flooding back. Could I trust the Lord
at this point? How could I help but trust one who had died
and given himself to save me from my sin? Twenty-five
years before, as an airman in HM Forces, I had come to
realise the emptiness of my life and yet how full it was
of sin. Clean-up campaigns had failed. They were all my
own efforts and a waste of time. But after hearing of
God's grace and power to save I was converted. Christ
became my Saviour. I knew that the God who had
promised to guide me as far as death and beyond would
not fail me now. And I could rest assured that he had
Mum's welfare in his perfect plan too.

The day came, early in the spring of 1993, when I had
to make the phone call and I needed direction from
Scripture. I had been reading through the Old Testament, from Genesis to Malachi from January to
December, a few chapters a day, following a plan. My
appointed reading for that day was Deuteronomy chapters one and two. When I reached chapter one verses six,
seven and eight the tears began to flow. 'The LORD our
God spake unto us in Horeb, saying, Ye have dwelt long
enough in this mount: Turn you, and take your journey,
go ... in the plain, in the hills, and in the vale, and in the
south, and by the sea-side. ... Behold, I have set the land
before you ...'. Having shared the verses with Ruth I
made the phone call.

We went as a family to Barnstaple for the Easter
weekend and just a few weeks later, in May, the church
members issued me with a call to the pastorate. We felt
it was the Lord's will for us to go and he confirmed it

and assured us over and over again as we read our Bibles.

I can look back to many occasions in our marriage when we have needed direction and have found it in the Word of God. Ruth and I met when I was in the Royal Air Force serving in Germany. She was visiting her parents who were serving the Lord there. It was, I suppose, a 'whirlwind romance' - not something we find it easy to talk about when we speak to young people's groups on 'relationships'! That was 1970. Believing God meant us to be together we were married the same year. We still believe it!

Twenty three years on, in 1993, Ruth and I received tremendous encouragement from the children. Charlotte, then 20, Simon 18, Fraser 15 and Abigail 13 no doubt had their own private thoughts and feelings concerning the impending move. They too found God speaking to them through his Word and what they shared of that is stored in our hearts. Angelina's reaction was sheer excitement!

A real peace possessed us during those early days as we shared the news with family and friends, particularly with those in our own church. Some saw it as an answer to prayer. Some did not. While we fully appreciated the advice and counsel of Christian friends, what do you do when this counsel conflicts? Nothing? Stand still? We knew that the ultimate guidance is from God and is to be found in his infallible Word. One day, when we have to account for our actions, we will not be able to hide behind the advice of friends when we have not heeded the counsel of God.

Ruth's view

My mother also was a great encouragement. She exhorted us to put God and his work first before everything else. I can still hear her say, 'Don't say "no" because of me.' Although my heart ached at the thought of leaving her to the care of others in the church, I was overwhelmed by the friends who offered to help, thus making it easier for me to let go. It was my turn to have my trust tested. My mind went back a couple of years to David's comment, 'Perhaps we won't go until the Lord takes Mum home.' I struggled with guilty feelings about leaving her and what people would think.

Thinking so much about Mum reminded me of the blessing I had had of a Christian home and upbringing. I was particularly grateful for a godly mother who, despite the busy-ness of being a missionary wife, always had time for my sister and me. We learnt such a lot from her selfless life and quiet faithfulness to Christ. It was against that background that, as a little girl of seven, I asked the Lord Jesus to forgive me my sins. He did. And he has gone on forgiving me ever since.

As I struggled to sort out my responsibilities to my ageing mother, a verse in my daily Bible reading spoke directly to me: Peter said to him (Jesus), 'We have left everything to follow you!' (Mark 10:28). And part of the comment in the notes that followed read, 'Yes, Lord, I did hear thy call; but my mother is in the road, my wife, my self-interest, and I can go no further ...'. I was reminded that God was in control and was encouraged to trust my mother to his care.

God makes no mistakes. A few weeks later, at the end of a happy holiday in London with my sister, the Lord took my mother home to be with himself in heaven. Eight weeks later, on the date set, we moved to North Devon.

God did not decide to take Mum home because we chose to move to Devon. Our Heavenly Father makes these decisions as he prepares his plans for us. And his plans are perfect. He has no need to look them up, check them or change them. I was reassured when I read God's words in Jeremiah 29:11: 'I know the plans I have for you,' declares the Lord. We found, as we had found before, that obeying God's will and following his plan can sometimes be painful. His plans for us as a family were full of changes in the summer and autumn of 1993.

Moving to Devon meant leaving two children behind. Charlotte stayed in Swindon to complete her nurse training and Simon went off to university in Bristol. We are amazed when we realise that the call to Barnstaple, my mother's homecall to heaven, saying goodbye to two children, moving house with all the natural apprehension of a new job, schools and town, all took place within the space of three months! Simon and Fraser would add 'not to mention GCSEs and A-levels' to this list! Both boys had exams on the day Granny died. We have proved again that God is able, well able, to cope with us and all that concerns us. As some of these events are fairly recent we know that we are not looking back through rose-tinted spectacles.

And now, eight months on, we have a garden to dig

again. As our kind friends in the church here wish the
manse to be bigger, they have engaged a builder to add
an extension. Drainpipes are being laid, soil shifted and
bricks and sand arrive daily. When the work is done we
will once again clear debris and establish a garden. But
we have a spiritual garden to tend too. Our home is
surrounded by a large estate where we will plant the seed
of the gospel and tend it. We look forward to blooms and
blossoms of new life appearing, and fruit too, as the
years go by. We trust in God, who has helped us until
now, to give the harvest.

11

ELMA ALEXANDER

Why am I crying?

It is May 1948 and in the warm sunshine the beech leaves are unfolding to that delicate pale green which lasts but a few days and releasing their rich perfume that can only be experienced and refuses all attempts at being described. Reaching up I pull a branch towards me and, burying my face in the leaves, I sob, 'What if I never see you or touch you again?' At thirteen years old, I did not understand the fear that gripped me. But it was soon forgotten.

The memory of that moment only returned the following spring - by which time I was severely crippled by a form of arthritis known as 'Still's Disease' and house-bound, as being moved was unbearably painful.

I was affected by arthritis periodically during my childhood and had been told by doctors that I would probably 'grow out of it'. Indeed, when I reached thirteen, after it seemed to vanish for a year, I thought this acceleration to virtual immobility would pass. But a few years later I was no longer able even to sit up. It had obviously come to stay.

Somehow I had already become used to living with it. Being by nature a shy person, I was very self-conscious of my twisted limbs and for a long time refused to see anyone except a few close relatives and friends. I never asked God 'Why me?' nor felt bitter, but I did question why my parents should have to agonise over this apparent tragedy affecting their only child.

Although my mother was a committed Christian she married an atheist. And my affliction only served to affirm my father's conviction that there was no God. I thought I was a Christian. After all, I had attended Sunday School as a child and continued to 'pray' each night. But somehow reading the Bible and talking about it held no attraction for me.

Climbing several Everests

I enjoyed writing to a number of pen-friends but it became frustrating having to dictate all my letters to my parents for them to write on my behalf. So, with a pencil tied to a long cane which I could grip in my already bent fingers, I attempted to write on a piece of paper pinned to a vertical board - as I lay the only way possible, flat on my back. The excitement of spelling out E-L-M-A in 2 inch high letters could not have been greater had I reached the top of Everest! With practice I mastered normal sized writing and then began sketching, something which I had loved doing as a child. By then I was 24.

About this time I got another cane with a 'tapper' on the end which I used to operate the keys of an old typewriter. Soon my days were filled with writing letters and sketching - plus some reading, having found that if small books were fixed on to my vertical table, I could turn the pages with yet another cane, on the end of which was a rubber. Although by this time all my joints were locked, except for a slight movement in one arm, it seemed that the more ideas I had of how to do things myself, the more I wanted to find others!

Jo Stafford, the American singer, had an appreciation club in London and through my membership of it I gained confidence in communicating with people and became able to face 'strangers'. Some of my pen-friends from England and abroad even came on holiday to visit me. A few of them have remained my dearest and closest friends to this day. Jo Stafford herself spent an afternoon with me when visiting Scotland in 1964. How I treasure that memory. Through my love of her God-given voice I was to meet people who helped change my life. I even found the love of a good man who shared more than ten years of his life with me - but therein lies another story!

My love of Country music has grown over the years. Although it is mainly secular many artists are Christians and use their music to express their faith and make public testimonies. Two in particular have been real inspirations: George Hamilton IV sings not only in concerts but in churches and prisons too; and Dominic Kirwan whose friendship has been a blessing to me. Perhaps following Country music is not an immediately obvious way of serving the Lord, but even in this I feel he fulfils one of my favourite texts: 'In all things God works for the good of those who love him, who have been called according to his promise' (Romans 8:28).

In 1966, a social worker suggested that I try to paint! I thought he was being more than a little unreasonable.

'I'd get more paint on myself than on the picture!' was my reply. He arrived a few days later with a little easel, a palette, some tubes of paint and brushes. The brushes were firmly fixed on to yet more canes. Putting a small piece of hardboard on the easel and some colours on the palette, he left me to it. Not wishing to seem ungrateful, I thought the least I could do was to prove to him that he had wasted his time! To my amazement it almost seemed as if my small movement on the brush was being guided by an unseen hand and the result was a recognisable scene.

Before long I was selling paintings to friends, had a local exhibition and graduated to using real canvas and oils. Thereafter I worked mainly on commissions, having been featured on local TV and in various newspapers. Still very self-conscious about my disability, I felt that what I was doing might encourage other disabled people. Over a period of some twelve years I created about 200 paintings, mostly of landscapes and animals.

Jesus found me

A Christian friend spoke to me occasionally over the years about his faith but I tended to change the subject, until one day he asked, 'If you die tonight, Elma, where will you go?' His question stunned me. I gathered my thoughts and said I hoped I would go to heaven. 'I don't hope I will,' he assured me, 'I know I will.' No more was said, but his certainty about his future made a deep impact on me and I felt a craving to read the Bible and learn more about Jesus.

Beginning with the New Testament, I read the whole Bible, and the more I read the more engrossed I became. This took over a year, at the end of which the enormity of what Christ had really done reached me, and on November 15th 1972 I was 'born again' by the power of the Holy Spirit and committed my life to the Lord. My conversion brought the greatest joy to my dear mother and my father's heart was touched too. It was only then that I realised just how the Lord had directed my life, even when I had ignored him. I wrote this little song to express how I felt then. I feel the same now, and always will.

Jesus found me
A poor losing sinner
Jesus found me
And made me a winner

He took my sin -
He saved my soul
And just for me -
He gave His all

Jesus found me
And with His forgiving
He has cleansed me
And life is worth living

I'm happy now -
And life is bliss
Now I am free -
I tell you this

Jesus found me -
And I am His

Being an only child raised in the Fife countryside during the war years I was very shy and the animals and birds, even the trees, were my companions. As I entered my teens I began to feel resentful of my parents' over-protectiveness and believe that, but for the intervention of my affliction, I would have left home and gone down paths on which I might never have met my Lord. On that spring morning, as I spoke to the trees I loved, perhaps the Lord cried with me because he knew what lay ahead.

My mother, caring for me without nursing help, believed in her lovely old-fashioned way that if she failed to do so I would be put into a home. Since I too believed this, I was terrified of losing her. Yet, when she died after a short illness in 1975, the Lord gave me that peace that passes all understanding. Father was unable to look after me alone, but my heavenly Father supplied home helps and nurses to care for me. I joined Anstruther Baptist Church and, because I could not be immersed, the pastor and deacons gathered in my room and there I was baptised by water being sprinkled on my head and made my public commitment as a Christian.

I had been spiritually healed and knew that the Lord could also physically heal me, *if* it was his will. For a time I did quite expect that to happen. However, through circumstances God clearly showed me that this was not to be, and his words in 2 Corinthians 12:9, 'My grace is sufficient for you, for my power is made perfect in weakness,' fulfilled their promise.

The smell of beech leaves

Soon afterwards my arthritis 'burned out' and left my joints locked but without inflammation. As long as my body remained in its prone position I no longer had the pain of earlier years. In all this time I had never left my room, but I now felt that if a rigid stretcher could be made for me I could cope with being carried outside. My first outing took place on another warm May day in 1978 and I lay under another beech tree where once again I could see and smell the leaves.

I will never forget that day and how acutely aware I was of everything around me: the heat of the sun and slight breeze on my face, the sounds of birds singing and trees rustling, and especially the smells of nature. Over them all was the scent of new beech leaves! I imagine entering heaven will be like that day. My one regret was that my mother was not there to share it with me. It reduced my father to tears.

Trains, boats and planes

Everyone thought that getting outside would allow my painting to develop further, but the Lord seemed to show me that stage of my life was over and he had other things for me to do. At first it appeared to be all for my pleasure. Because I was able to lie in an estate car friends took me to church and for drives around the countryside. I even got to concerts.

When friends in Epsom invited me to spend Christmas with them I travelled there by train, lying on my stretcher in the guard's van! The next summer saw me migrating south like the birds, and in the years that followed I holidayed with friends in various parts of England. I also went on some boat trips - with my stretcher lashed to the front of the wheelhouse! Having been on 'trains and boats' my remaining ambition was 'planes' - so Physically Handicapped & Able Bodied (PHAB) arranged for me to be taken up in a small aeroplane and flown over Fife. That was a magnificent experience. Flying down the Firth of Forth the pilot banked the plane so that I could see the villages on the Fife coast below. What a thrill it was to be able to recognise them from an angle in the sky!

More new beginnings
I continued to do a lot of typing but longed for a computer and one materialised in 1984 through the organisation Linking Education and Disability (LEAD). After gaining my 'O' Level and Advanced Computer Programming Certificates through the Open Learning Scheme at Glenrothes Technical College, I wrote educational software programmes for a local school. Now I use my computer for church work, particularly as editor of my congregational magazine, and also for charitable fundraising.

I have always enjoyed composing poetry. In my younger days it was mostly light-hearted doggerel, but after becoming a Christian I no longer found satisfaction in 'making up' rhymes. Instead I find I get sudden spells of inspiration during which I write down all the words that pour into my head. Many months may pass between bursts of poetry writing. I resist any temptation to 'improve' them and often they make no sense to me at all, yet other people who read them find something in my poems for them. Because of this I don't discard my writings.

One poem which has been especially used to speak to people about God's providence was inspired by the haar, the sea mist that from time to time rolls along the east coast of Scotland like a carpet of cloud.

> In the Haar
> The world is so still
> So silent
> No sky
> No horizon
> Only vague shapes staring
> Through the gloom.
>
> In the Haar
> An echo beckons
> From deep in my soul
> Something stirs
> Awakes
> A forgotten memory
> Lost in the eternity of time
>
> In the Haar
> Before the world was massed
> Before creation began
> Even then my God knew me
> And planned me
> And loved me
> In the Haar

At Easter 1990, I gave my pastor a poem I had written called *The Tree*. He passed it to the chairman of the Scottish Fellowship of Christian Writers who suggested that I might like to become a member. I did not consider myself qualified to use the title 'writer' but did feel an urge to join, thinking it might help me improve my secular writing as I enjoy sending letters and small articles to the press. As I write this account of God's dealings with me I am hoping to attend my third SFCW Conference. How grateful I am that the Lord led me to join: not only has it helped my writing but I have found new friends in the members. It is at the request of one of them that I am writing this chapter for the book she is editing and you are reading!

I have overcome my self-consciousness at being seen in public and am intrigued by the different ways in which people react when encountering me for the first time! Some very obviously pretend they have not seen me, but most just stare, unsure of what to do. On these occasions I always do the same thing - I smile at them! This usually prompts one of two reactions, either they look startled and hurry off in the opposite direction, or they smile back. A smile is sometimes followed by them coming to me and talking, and the conversation often ends with a comment about how much they have been inspired or helped by meeting me. I am quick to put them right - there is no credit due to me, all that I achieve is done in the strength of the Lord. One person expressed it like this, 'I've seen many Christians praising God but felt it was alright for them, they had nothing to complain about. But when someone in your circumstances can still praise the Lord, then I can believe there is something in it.'

At home with Benjie

My father died in 1980 and although I knew it was not practical to live alone in an isolated house I was very reluctant to leave my beloved country home. I had lived there all my life. Eventually, three years later, I felt led to move to the little semi-detached house in Crail, still in the beautiful East Neuk of Fife, where I now live very happily with my much loved cat Benjie. For fourteen years he has been one of the Lord's most precious gifts to me.

So how, a reader may be asking, does someone as immobile as I am manage to live alone when, after all, I cannot even feed myself. My answer to that would have to be, 'Where the Lord guides, the Lord provides!' And here is how he has done it. I have three lovely home carers. On weekdays they come in at breakfast, lunch and tea times and each takes a turn at doing all three meals at weekends. They also do my housework and shopping. A nurse calls in the morning to wash and dress me and every evening a 'tuck-in' nurse comes to give me supper and settle me for the night. These girls are very different but they are equally caring so I think of them more as friends than official medical staff. Using my Attendance Allowance I employ someone for a few hours each week to do all the 'little' things like closing letters, watering my plants and taking me out to the garden on nice days.

That covers the practicalities of my care, but what, I am sometimes asked, about all those long hours on my own. Long - that's a laugh! Time goes past much too quickly with the help of Mr POSSUM and the wonders of modern technology. In 1961 a telephone engineer, Frank Holmes, adapted my telephone by putting the receiver on a stand at my ear and a tiny switch under my right elbow which connected me to incoming callers and allowed me to make outgoing calls through the operator.

The following year he expanded the idea and produced a box called 'ELMA 2' (Electronic Mechanical Aid). This allowed me to switch on and off a light, my radio and television, the room heater and a door intercom system - all with a little press of my elbow! Frank's invention was later taken on by the Disabled Unit at Stoke Mandeville Hospital and it has now become the refined POSSUM (Patient Operated Selector Switching Unit Mechanism) which is supplied by the Health Board. This unit has increased my independence yet further as I can use it to open and close the curtains, dial telephone numbers without going through the operator, and put my computer and printer on and off. I still use my long cane. With it I operate my computer keyboard and the remote controls which allow me to select radio and television channels and also give me access to videos, cassettes and compact disks. The choice is mine.

While I am totally dependent on other people I feel a great sense of independence and control of my life. But I am very aware that the real control is in the hands of my kind and loving Lord. He has brought me such a long way since that May day in 1948 and the tears I shed under the beech tree. Three young trees in my garden in Crail have grown from seedlings from the ones outside my old home in the country. I still cannot reach up to touch them - but they often seem to give me a very knowing nod!

Yes, I would rather be a disabled Christian serving the Lord than be physically fit without him. One advantage of lying on my back is that I can only look up. He is always there and no longer the distant God of my youth, but close beside me and watching over me. I could not have coped with my situation without him. My heavenly Father has brought me through many bad patches, given me so many good times, and we still have a wonderful future to share.

12

KEITH JONES

Life as an adventure

Although I am now in my forties I am still young at heart. I love adventure, and when I talk about the thrills and challenges I've met my pulse races, and my voice does too. Perhaps it was that sense of adventure which made me join the Royal Navy and led to my being a pilot, not of a boat at sea, but of an aircraft as a member of 899 Naval Air Squadron and later 849 Naval Air Squadron serving on board HMS Ark Royal.

My wife, Lin, looked at life in the same way. When we met something which was difficult or frightening, or just new and unknown, we got into the habit of calling it an adventure. Somehow that softened the edges of hard things, taking the thought of danger out of situations but still keeping the sense of excitement. It did something else too. It gave us a feeling of oneness. What we were doing we were doing together. What we were facing, we were not facing alone.

Lin had been converted in our courting days in 1970 through a Christian couple who led her to the Lord. I did not share her faith. When we married I was front line flying in a fighter squadron. The following year, while I was at home recovering from a leg injury, two young fellow officers invited us to join them at a harvest thanksgiving service in their church. We went along and found a warmth and fellowship I had never experienced before. There was real loving care and concern for members and visitors alike. As time passed we found ourselves going to church four times a week even though my leg was still in plaster! Lin was faithful in prayer for me and nine months later, in October 1971, I committed my life to the Lord. I was 25 years old when I became a Christian.

For the first four years of my commission I was not a believer and for the last four, when I was based at Lossiemouth in Moray, I was. Some radical changes took place in my life, especially in my behaviour and language. It was very interesting to see the reaction of the people with whom I had drunk and messed around. Some of them did not like the changes that had taken place, but others did.

Where do we go from here?
As my time in the navy came to an end we wondered what God's plans for us were. Because the Lord had put a love of people in our hearts we considered doing some sort of social work. Lin was already a trained nursery nurse. But social work did not seem right for us. It was during this time of indecision that a mission was held in our church in Elgin. Our thinking was all wrong when we went to the Saturday evening meeting. Get all the 'pagans' in, we thought, stick them in the pews and get them converted. Instead we heard the preacher speaking to us, the believers, urging us to really commit ourselves

to the Lord. That night, quite independently of each other, we told God that whatever he wanted us to do we would do. I believe that he lodged that promise in heaven and one day not long afterwards prompted us both, again independently, towards the mission field.

Our family situation was uncomplicated, from the point of view of a mission society, as we were childless. This was in a sense another adventure, though a hard one, for Lin loved children but could not have any. As friends and family had babies Lin's heart broke. She was not bitter nor was she jealous, just deeply troubled. We prayed about it and asked the Lord to help and he did, enabling Lin to overcome her hurt and heartbreak. As a child Lin had major surgery because of kidney trouble. She was X-rayed many times, and was also affected by X-rays while accompanying children with whom she worked, until a doctor warned her of the dangers of over-exposure. But it was probably too late. Damage had already been done.

We were so naive in our approach to guidance that looking back I wonder at the simplicity of our understanding. But the Lord had marked out a way for us and we walked in it. And the way was studded with adventure. We applied to, and were accepted by, Mission Aviation Fellowship. Our cottage in the lovely Morayshire village of Garmouth sold and we found ourselves instead in one small room in the Brixham YMCA in London while I studied for my commercial pilot's licence. God must have smiled as he planned our next home - a great big bungalow back in Scotland situated in half an acre of landscaped garden. We never knew what was coming next!

What we were planning for was a three year period of service in Ethiopia. But Ethiopia closed up and we were redirected to All Nations Christian College where we spent a year studying, learning and having many more rough edges knocked off. During that academic year we discovered that the Lord had called people into his service who were very different denominationally, culturally and in personality - quite an eye-opener to two very young Christians. So the summer of 1977 did not find me flying an MAF plane in Ethiopia, instead I worked as a pilot flying pleasure flights around Great Yarmouth, a short summer job that provided ideal experience with light aircraft before going overseas.

To Chad via Paris

The next part of God's plan unfolded. It was another adventure, a really difficult one, especially for Lin who was not a natural linguist. We had to spend six months in Paris learning French. It was a relief for her when we came back for six months in the UK at the end of which, on 5th January 1979, we left for Chad, flying via Paris. We were clueless! Mosquito nets were a mystery to us. And not only had we to speak French, but when we went shopping we had to argue in it in order to buy anything! It was either that or pay four times the true value.

Our first few weeks in Chad were marvellous. Everything was new and exciting - the Africans, the Arabs, the dancing, the smells, sights and sounds of the place - it was lovely. And that short period became

especially precious because within weeks of our arrival
civil war broke out and we found ourselves in the thick
of it, literally. Bombs fell about us, and shots rang out
in our ears, but the Lord kept us, and those with whom
we were working, safe. After the first two weeks of
heavy fighting relative peace returned enabling us to
continue normal MAF operations. Flying in Chad was
exciting as most of it was spent on medical tournées,
carrying doctors to where they were most needed and
patients to where they could best be helped. Lin worked
as the radio operator, flight following and keeping in
regular touch with the pilots.

When civil war erupted again it became clear that we,
along with all other expatriates, should leave Chad, but
not before we had seen, and been involved in, some quite
awful situations. Much though we loved the country and
the people, it was a relief to leave and spend six months
working in Nairobi, Kenya, before moving on to Sudan.
Rather than use an airline we went by road, crossing the
Kenyan / Sudanese border in our little Suzuki jeep on
Christmas Day 1979 to begin the New Year in a new
adventure there. Seeing 'life in the Lord' as an adventure
helped us through the three years we spent in Sudan. It
was a really hard time that saw many tears and much
heartache.

A new home - on wheels
Our time with MAF abroad came to an end in March
1983 when the Lord led us to work with MAF at home.
Our chosen job was to travel the length and breadth of

the country taking meetings and speaking about the work of the Fellowship. Having no home of our own meant that our private life was limited to the confines of our car. We stayed with people as their guests wherever we found ourselves visiting. That was alright for a short time but produced its own problems. From time to time we found ourselves in situations where there was tension in a family and, while we were not part of it, we were right in the middle of it. 'If we are going to be doing this work for any length of time,' we said, 'let's get ourselves a caravan.' And the Lord provided one for us just then. Someone gave a caravan to MAF and it became our very own little home on wheels, towed by a converted ambulance, suitably equipped, which was our mobile office and transport.

In October 1983 we started travelling, like snails we were told, with our home on our back! The work was great fun and we especially appreciated the privacy the caravan enabled us to have. It was a haven to us wherever we went.

Hard times ahead

On a visit to Dublin Lin became unwell with a cold which became flu. She did not seem able to shake it off. Our itinerary took us from Ireland to Wales where Lin grew worse and could not attend the meetings scheduled for us. I left her in the caravan while I fulfilled our speaking engagements, then returned to look after her in the evenings. We got as far as Bristol where a group of friends met together to pray for her. For a time she seemed quite a bit better, but when we went back to Folkestone and the headquarters of Mission Aviation Fellowship, Lin became ill again.

I had to leave her behind while I continued to work, but when I came back and she had not improved we went to our own doctor who arranged a blood test. Lin had Acute Myeloid Leukaemia and was told she had just four weeks to live. That was on 15th June 1984. After giving us the news the doctor left us for a little while to talk together. Lin was as white as a sheet because of the state of her blood and her illness. She took me by the hand, smiled and said, 'Another adventure, Keith.' I remember the look on her face. There was uncertainty but no fear. I didn't know what to say.

The following day I drove to Lin's parents, told them the news and brought them back to see her. She had had a blood transfusion and was looking fresh and bright. Having prayed for her parents for years Lin then took them by their hands, 'Mum and Dad,' she said, 'I've got four weeks to live and I know where I'm going. You don't. Can I ask you to consider the Lord during this time?' And while Lin was ill they both became believers.

Chemotherapy was explained to us and we were advised that it would be appropriate for Lin. The alternative was to do nothing and allow her to die. She went through some awful times, then one day my office phone rang and when I answered it I heard a little voice say, 'Keith, I'm in remission. It's all over.' Lin came home to our caravan and was kept on maintenance treatment with a view to having a bone marrow transplant at the beginning of the following year. We scraped up £1,000 for a deposit and put it down on a little flat near MAF's office in Folkestone. Lin needed somewhere comfortable and quiet, and with no noisy neighbours, to allow her to regain her strength. But she did not see our flat for more than a few weeks.

Lin's treatment then followed the course that had been outlined to us - intensive radiotherapy and a bone marrow transplant with its long, drawn out, but necessary, follow-up regime. For a while there was hope that she was going to get better, then Lin entered a really bad patch and as time passed her life became a nightmare. She suffered from repeated infections and for a time reacted to her medication by being quite mentally disturbed. Eventually infections caused Lin to lose her sight and hearing.

On one occasion when she was allowed home Lin developed an infection and I had to rush her back to hospital. It was one o'clock in the morning and the car would not start. I remember pushing and pushing it. My strength could only have come from God for I pushed the 'old banger' with Lin sitting in it round the flat streets of Folkestone for a mile before finding a hill steep enough to allow it to start. I was so drenched with sweat I must have looked as though I had stepped right out of a bath.

I drove Lin to London and she was admitted to an isolation ward. I remember her looking at me. She was scarcely recognisable. Lin was reduced to skin and bone and neither knew where she was nor what she was saying. 'Keith,' she said, 'get out of my life. I don't want to see you again.' I knew that was not Lin speaking but the result of all that was happening to her. The hallucinations and nightmares from which she suffered made Lin believe she was going to hell and she thought she might take me with her. I told her I would go home but come back the next day to see her. 'Don't bother,' she replied. Looking round at her I wept. She was so ill, so changed. My Lin was hardly recognisable. Then I called as loudly as I could, 'I can't leave you.' I threw my arms around her, helped her unpack, then an hour later left her ... asleep. I cried all the way home.

Towards the end of 1985 Lin developed an infection of the brain and on 15th December she died, aged 43. When I think back to that time there are great chunks of my life of which I have no recollection at all, while other things feel as yesterday.

God in the midst of it all

Some time later, after Lin had died, the Lord reminded me of that night. I heard him speaking to me in my mind and heart telling me that there was a time in eternity when his Son took on his shoulders the sin of the world and carried it to Golgotha where he was nailed to the cross for my sins and the sins of others too. In those moments God showed me that when he looked at his Son Jesus with all the violence and hatred and murder and every other evil heaped upon him he was also unrecognisable. And that while he looked at him and could have gone to him, thrown his arms around him, embraced him and told him he would never leave him, he did not. He turned his back on his own dear Son Jesus and left him there to pay the death penalty for my sin.

I realised in that experience that what Lin and I went through was no more than a glimpse of the pain God endured so to give his Son Jesus Christ. He drew apart the curtain that separates man from the sufferings of Christ just a little and allowed me to look in. That experience has helped me to understand perhaps more than most people what the great truth of salvation meant to God. And it has enabled me to share with others in a more informed way something of his costly love for them.

So Lin completed her last adventure on earth and went on to that greatest adventure of all - seeing God in all his glory in heaven and being welcomed home by the Lord whom she had loved and served. For me the adventure was different. I had to learn to walk through the valley of the shadow of death. When Lin died I thought I had reached rock bottom but I had not. The awful depression that followed has affected me to a greater or lesser degree from time to time ever since.

When I went back to work after Lin's death I found it impossible to preach. It just was not in me to do it. Stuart King, MAF's Chief Executive, invited me to produce reports on the mission's work overseas and organise its fund-raising activities. Mission Aviation Fellowship's work is capital intensive because of the cost of aircraft, hangers and so on. The Lord's help and grace have enabled me to raise several million pounds from a range of organisations both on mainland Europe and in the United Kingdom.

During a brief time away from MAF working with an organisation which helped children with cancer, I was asked to return. Initially I said no. But when a second invitation came and was confirmed in my Bible reading that same day, I agreed and went back while continuing to work for a time with the children's charity on a voluntary basis.

I was asked to become MAF's Director of Development. In terms of charity work development includes raising funds, encouraging and informing supporters and reaching out to others who might become interested, inspiring people to pray for the work of the Fellowship, and much more. In practical terms this means collecting and collating information, and producing progress reports, MAF News and a whole range of other things.

On 14th February 1994 MAF UK and MAF Europe split. MAF UK now sits alongside the other mainland European groups as a resourcing organisation for MAF Europe, providing the people, the prayer and the finance necessary for its work. MAF Europe is the operational side of the organisation. When I was invited to become Chief Executive of MAF UK I agreed to accept the post. And that's where I am now, working alongside a tremendous team of experienced men and women.

Personal blessings

God has not confined his blessings to my working life. In his grace and wisdom he brought Ruth and me together. She, in her own way, had also been 'through the mill'. I trust I have been an encouragement to her. She certainly has been to me. We were married in 1987 and two years later Ruth and I had a son, David. He's a lovely little fellow, but very tiring. I suppose all five-year-olds are. With what energy Ruth has left over when David has done with her, she works from time to time as a writer with MAF and does a useful and necessary job in preparing the prayer diary.

My life has had its adventures. Some have been fun and some hard, dreadfully hard. But God, who planned the path along which I have walked thus far, holds my future, my family's future, and the future of Mission Aviation Fellowship securely in his hands. I am content to leave it there.